GUIDING YOURSELF
INTO A
SPIRITUAL REALITY

REVISED EDITION

Tolly Burkan
and
Peggy Dylan Burkan

REUNION PRESS
TWAIN HARTE, CALIFORNIA

Cover Photography: Brian Garland

REVISED EDITION
ISBN 0-935616-09-8

Library of Congress No. 83-91310

Copies of this book may be obtained through your local bookstore. Copies are available by mail from REUNION PRESS, Box 1738, Twain Harte, CA 95383. Please add $1.50 for postage and handling. California residents add 36¢ for sales tax.

Guiding Yourself Into A Spiritual Reality has an accompanying workbook that can be ordered from REUNION PRESS. The workbook is $6.95 plus $1.50 for postage and handling. California residents add 42¢ for sales tax.

PRINTING HISTORY

First Printing: March, 1984	3,000 copies
Second Printing: June, 1984	10,000 copies
Third Printing: September, 1984	10,000 copies

Manufactured in the United States of America
REUNION PRESS, INC.
BOX 1738
TWAIN HARTE, CA 95383

Preface

❧

About
Firewalking

This book is not about firewalking. We truly do not understand the physical phenomenon and we leave scientists with the job of discovering why it is possible. So far, there are only theories available, but no bottom-line explanation. It is fine with us that some mystery remain in the universe. Our only interest in firewalking is to use it as a tool to help people find their hidden potential. And that is what this book is about: developing **your** potential as a human being. Firewalking has become a symbol which reminds us that being a mere human is not so "mere."

We possess an ability to tap a reservoir of magic that most people do not even know exists. Firewalking, more than anything else perhaps, reveals that all we have heard may only be a **hint** of the miraculous nature of this universe we call home.   After people walk on hot coals measured at over 1200° F. they usually find all kinds of wonderful changes happening in their lives: improvement in health, relationships, jobs, etc. Yet as one sage of antiquity put it, "Blessed are those who see miracles and believe, but more blessed are those who see no miracles and still believe".

Although 25,000 Americans have walked on fire in the last two years, that still represents only a small percentage of the population. The firewalk is like a magnet; it brings people to us so they can discover what it is we have to share. Our message is simple: **Be all you can be.** Our desire is to serve people by assisting them to overcome limitations in all areas of their lives.

All the information we provide in our Firewalking Workshops is contained in this book. More people can have access to the information by reading the book than by physically attending a firewalk. This book and the accompanying workbook can bring you all the power, joy and spirit that people discover in firewalking.

After all, life itself can often be a "firewalk". This book will assist you in crossing **that** fire without getting burned.

Dedicated
to
The Transformation of the Planet

ACKNOWLEDGMENTS

Many people have helped shape the ideas in this book; it is impossible to thank them all. However, the authors would like to specifically acknowledge Sathya Sai Baba, Richard Alpert, Ken Keyes, Werner Erhard and Albert Einstein for their words, guidance and inspiration. Also, special gratitude goes to Hilda Charlton for her constant love, teaching and support.

CONTENTS

Introduction   9
PART ONE: BASIC INFORMATION
1 Five Points of Power   13
2 Human Games   21
3 Expanding Your Mind   27
4 Seven Life Requirements   37
5 Setting Intentions   49
6 Affirmations   57
7 Invisible Guidance   61
8 Transforming Human Experience   67
9 Four Stages of Growth   75

PART TWO: APPLICATIONS
10 Overcoming Fear and Limiting Beliefs   85
11 Living in Relationship   93
12 Merging with God through *Tantra*   99
13 Penetrating the Illusion   111
14 Serving Yourself by Serving Others   121
An Invitation
Suggested Reading

*You will get more from reading this book if
you use the accompanying workbook as well.*

INTRODUCTION

The most exciting magic show we can witness is to observe our own transformation. If you have been on the path of self-development for any length of time, you have probably seen yourself go through many changes. The game of spiritual evolution never ends.

The purpose of this pocket-guide is to assist you in focusing on where your next step of growth lies. It will create movement in areas where you feel stuck and speed up progress in whatever direction you are already moving.

If you have not yet discovered the magic of self-awareness, this guidebook could very likely change your entire life. It will show you how to transmute each and every day into a spiritual reality. If you follow the guidelines in this book, there will no longer be any such thing as an "ordinary" moment in your life.

You are an incredible, God-like being whose only limitation is the way in which you perceive yourself and the reality in which you live. You possess the potential to obtain whatever you desire. Most people falter on the path of success mainly because they lack a clear sense of where they *really* want to go. *Guiding Yourself into a Spiritual Reality* will assist you in getting clear on what you really want so you can begin manifesting it right now.

You are about to explore a manual that will show you how to release mental stress, unblock constricted energy, create greater sensitivity, enhance your relationships and add to your health, relaxation and sense of well-being. Today more than ever before, individuals are delving beyond the familiar states of mind to discover their fullest potential. This handbook contains practical methods and procedures which will give you the tools to make radical changes in yourself starting this very minute.

Part One

BASIC INFORMATION

1

FIVE POINTS OF POWER

These Five Points of Power are things to do that will immediately enrich your life and produce an environment in which harmony and fulfillment can thrive.

FIVE POINTS OF POWER
1. Pay attention.
2. Speak the truth.
3. Ask for what you want.
4. Take responsibility for your experience.
5. Keep your agreements.

1. Pay attention. Learning how to pay attention is perhaps the most basic part of personal growth. The *Attentive Awareness* of which we are now speaking is not a casual state of mind. When we refer to *paying attention* as a Point of Power, we mean *paying attention 100%*. When you pay attention *completely,* life is transformed. When you pay attention to the smell of a flower 100%, you *become* the smell of the flower. When you pay attention 100% to the taste of food, you *become* the taste of food.

How often do you sit at the dinner table watching television and never tasting the meal you are eating? How frequently do you consume your dinner while thinking about the events of the day or worrying about appointments and bills? Only when you are not distracted can you fully experience the richness of the food in your mouth.

Here is a story which illustrates the power of paying attention. A *Zen* monk is hiking through the jungle when suddenly a tiger leaps in his path. The monk turns and flees until he finally comes to a steep cliff. Growing along the edge of the cliff is a long vine. He immediately descends the vine, but when he looks down, he discovers two tigers waiting for him at the base of the vine. Of course, by now, there are several tigers looking down at him from above. If that isn't enough, two mice are chewing through the vine.

Suddenly, the monk notices a wild strawberry growing from the side of the cliff. He plucks the strawberry and pops it into his mouth. The traditional story ends here. It is a *Zen* story and so it assumes that the listener will internally know the rest. Rather than stop now, however, let's look at the story's implications.

When the monk popped the strawberry into his mouth, he instantly paid attention to the taste of the strawberry. *He paid attention 100%!* When you pay attention 100% to the taste of food, you *become* the taste. Therefore, the monk *became* the strawberry and, of course, he never had an experience of being eaten by the tigers.

The story of the tigers and the strawberry is symbolic. Life is always sending us tigers and always sending us strawberries. For example, if you are a non-smoker and through a mix-up in your train reservation you find yourself in a smoke-filled car, you can easily create a hellish situation for yourself. You can blame, you can curse, you can regret—in short, you can suffer throughout the entire train ride. The smoky air can be the "tiger." If you do not wish to suffer, however, you can find a "strawberry" on which to focus your attention. Perhaps there is a glorious sunset you can watch through the window. If you focus your attention 100% on the sunset, you can instantly uplevel your experience from one of suffering to one of joy.

Life is always handing you "tigers" and always handing you "strawberries." It's up to you to choose what you want to experience. When you feel miserable, it's only because you are dwelling on the "tigers." At that moment, you have to find a "strawberry" and pay attention to *it* 100%. Remember, life is set up so that whenever a door is slammed shut, somewhere a window is left open.

Attentive Awareness is also described in this ancient tale about an old wiseman's son. Learned men from all corners of the earth would journey to see this wiseman and ask his advice. The son of the wiseman, however, was an impish fellow whose mischief was always causing upsets in the local community.

Finally, out of sheer frustration at his own inability to reach the boy, the wiseman sent his son to the king. The boy thus appeared before the monarch with the message that his father had sent him to the king hoping that the king could teach him where his father had failed.

The king pondered for a long while, since after all, he himself traveled often to consult the boy's father. How could he hope to teach the boy anything if the boy's own father had failed? Suddenly, the king was inspired. He looked around the huge hall and surveyed the belly dancers, the mountain of exotic food and the assembled musicians. After a moment of thought, the king snapped his fingers, which summoned two tall, muscular warriors.

The king ordered his two guards to stand on either side of the boy. He then placed a bowl of water on the youth's head. The bowl was filled to the brim. "Draw your swords," the sovereign commanded. "If this boy spills so much as one drop of water, you are to cut off his head immediately. Don't give him time to blink or utter one word. Now take him to the circus!"

So the guards and the boy went to the circus. Jugglers and clowns paraded among throngs of people, small children darted in all directions, merchants and food vendors hawked their wares. There were animals roaming about, musicians, dancers and acrobats. Do you think the boy noticed any of it? Of course not! All he was aware of was the bowl of water on his head. He learned to *pay attention*.

When you cultivate this same ability to focus your attention 100%, you will become your own best teacher. You will be able to learn from situations you never even noticed before. So many problems are just byproducts of not paying attention. Children spill milk as a result of not paying attention. Someone may fall down a flight of stairs because of not paying attention. Litter, war, pollution and prejudice are all a result of not paying attention. In fact, when you are behind the wheel of a car, paying attention can literally save your life. Paying attention to your thoughts will reveal how *you create* most of your problems. The first Point of Power—PAY ATTENTION!—is so important, that it will be continually mentioned throughout this book.

2. Speak the truth. Speaking the truth is more than just a social nicety. When you speak the truth as a commitment to your own growth, you actually align yourself with a tremendous power: *Truth*, with a capital "T." When you describe your feelings or relate something which you have experienced, you are speaking the truth. When you pass along gossip you are not necessarily speaking the truth. Words have an amazing amount of power and you should constantly be watchful to see that your words are of service to yourself and others.

When you speak about your own inner experience, your words will bring you closer to other people. This growing closer is a reflection of our instinctive love for sincerity. As you develop an ability to monitor what you say, you will discover that when you speak the truth you will feel better about yourself and your relationships with others. People will know you as having integrity and you will be regarded as someone who can be trusted. When you receive trust and respect, you tend to trust and respect others more easily and the entire quality of your day-to-day experience is enriched. Speaking the truth is ancient wisdom and its power has been known for thousands of years. As you align yourself with Truth, your self-esteem will grow and you will see it constantly reflected back in the way people relate to you.

3. Ask for what you want. You can instantly reap the benefit of this simple action. By verbalizing your wants and needs, you are certainly more likely to receive them than if you just play the role of a passive mute. At the table you may ask someone to pass the butter, yet feel reluctant to request a shoulder massage when a nagging ache is causing your upper back to cramp. Asking for what you want demonstrates a level of self-love which is far healthier than the unworthiness most people feel.

Before you can ask for what you want, of course, you must know what you want. You may be yearning for a relationship, but you might be too general. For instance, it is not good enough to simply say, "I want a woman in my life." You must be specific. What height is she? What are her likes? What color hair does she have? The more specific you are, the more likely you are to get what you want. This will later be covered in greater detail.

The power in asking for what you want doesn't just relate to speaking with other people. You can also ask "silently." Prayer, meditation, visualization and affirmations are all aspects of asking for what you want. The secret here is persistence. Without being demanding and without conditions, keep focusing on what you want. Ask for it. Don't torture yourself with impatience and don't make your happiness dependent on whatever it is you are asking for. You are making your needs and wants known. That is a step toward manifesting them.

This Point of Power may almost appear too simple. It seems so obvious. Yet, in many subtle ways, we overlook it completely. Some women never get the nurturing they desire from their husbands. There's no reason for them to be having this dilemma. All that is needed is for them to ask for what they want. "Stroke me here" or "Touch me like this" may be all the verbalization that it takes to bring about the results they desire. Do not underestimate the power in being able to *ask for what you want.*

4. Take responsibility for your experience. Too often, we think other people cause us to feel whatever it is that goes on inside us. "He made me angry" or "she makes my heart swell" are statements that deny how we create our own experience. External events are merely stimulating situations. We are free to choose our own response to those situations. You are not a robot who must automatically respond a certain way when a specific button is pushed. You are free to select whatever response you desire.

As soon as you give up blaming others, you can start seeing reality with a new perspective. Instead of saying, "He made me angry," you can rephrase your experience by saying, "When he does that, I am reminded of similar experiences from my past and I react with anger." In this way, you are *taking responsibility* for your experience. Stop creating yourself as a victim. All that does is constantly make you feel helpless. As soon as you start accepting personal responsibility, you will realize that you can change any experience *internally.* Fred or Jim can do or say whatever they please, but you do not have to respond any certain way. *You* make yourself angry; *you* make yourself happy. You are the master of your own life.

Depending on where each person was raised, ten people in the same room can have ten different reactions to a given situation. *Each person creates their experience based on their past.* No one can presume to know what another person is experiencing. We can only be sure of our own experience. Because we are humans, we also have the ability to transform any experience we have. For example, if you are not enjoying yourself, you can choose to *learn* and *grow* from that situation. *It is actually possible to use every circumstance for either pleasure or growth.* In this way, you can never again lose in life. When you are choosing to enjoy yourself or grow in every moment, life becomes a constant adventure, never a battle.

Once you take responsibility for your own experience, you will see how it is possible to change things in your life that you used to regret. The future suddenly will seem brilliant with infinite possibilities. You will be able to take control of your destiny and create whatever experiences you want.

5. Keep your agreements. Once you make a commitment to yourself to keep your agreements, your awareness will instantly notice whenever an agreement has been broken. For example, if you tell your friend that you will meet her at 4:30 and you do not arrive until 4:45, you will silently note that you have broken an agreement. You have created a small bump in what could have been a bumpless road. By setting an intention to *keep agreements,* you will see how much harmony or disharmony you are creating in your Universe. This may seem like a trivial point, yet when you are not respectful of even the most inconsequential agreement, the path of life can never be completely smooth.

These Five Points of Power represent a starting place on the journey into self-awareness. They are simple tools and create dramatic results. If you were to practice only these Five Points and never invest any more energy into your personal growth, you would still find a remarkable difference in your life. These five things alone can transform your day-to-day experience of living. They will contribute to your sense of well-being, they will improve your relationships with others and will assist you in becoming more alive, successful and prosperous.

2

HUMAN GAMES

Imagine a continent with a path winding its way from the southern shore toward the northern tip. We're going to use this image as we follow the development of human consciousness through some of the different games we play.

The path of consciousness often begins with a painful experience. This initial pain is symbolized by dark caves near the southern shore on this Continent of Human Games. Though your intention may be to walk a path of joy, it often takes pain to shake you out of your habitual ways of thinking and behaving. This motivating force can be the death of someone you love; it makes you question all your beliefs. The pain may result from an illness. It could be a psychological pain so deep that it forces you to look for other possibilities. Imagine an arrow on a bow. The archer draws the arrow back, straining the bow. That strain lets him know the arrow will fly with force. It's the same with initial pain. It builds the energy or motivation to carry us through hardships on the path. When the pain gets such that we can no longer bear it, we look for new possibilities. This leads to growth.

Most of your behavior and habitual ways of thinking were initially set in you by early childhood experiences and most of those experiences had survival implications attached to them. A child who is angrily told to modify its behavior will feel its survival depends on obeying the command. That command, when repeated often enough, becomes an internal law. When growth demands that you change your conditioning, an aspect of you will feel that your survival is being threatened and fear may result.

As you start to change and leave those Caves of Pain, you might next encounter the Forest of Fear. Fear is a chemical reaction that takes place to insure the survival of the body. When you feel your survival is threatened, fear rushes through you with the intention of protecting you through its physiological effects. So, as you become a more conscious being, be aware that you might find yourself in the Forest of Fear. For this reason, there is a chapter specifically about fear later in the book.

Past the forest, the path wends its way through a marsh. This is the Marsh of Resistance. Resistance, like a rock in a river, will slow you down. When you are changing too fast or encountering patterns you aren't ready to give up yet, resistance slows you down.

Resistance manifests itself in many forms. Some of the more common are body pains, boredom, anger, being over-talkative, or doing anything distracting. When you are experiencing resistance on the path, realize that something is frightening you. At such a time, reassure yourself and slow down a bit.

When we finally pull ourselves out of resistance and follow the path further up the continent, we come to a mountain: the Mountain of Effort. It seems large and foreboding. If it weren't for those Caves of Pain behind us, we'd probably turn back.

It took a lot of energy on the part of your schooling, your parents and yourself to program you in the way you've been programmed and it's going to take equal energy, if not more, for you to change. Remember that many of your patterns were established with the force of threatened survival, the strongest force in the animal kingdom. That energy is going to have to be counteracted with strong intention if you are to scale the Mountain of Effort. You have to be willing to put energy into your transformation.

As you grow in consciousness you may experience momentary setbacks. Surges of unexplainable emotion, lows following experiential highs, physical illness or other unusual body symptoms. This is a natural occurrence on the path and it is symbolized as the Pond of Ego Death. Remember that the patterns you are now transforming have lots of memories, thoughts and emotions associated with them. They represent blocked energy. When the pattern is changed, that energy is released, resulting in various symptoms. The symptoms of ego death are a natural feature on the path toward consciousness.

After traveling halfway up the continent you will come to an important area; it actually divides the continent in half. It is the River of Blame. Most people move from the Caves of Pain into fear, then resistance and then back to pain. They never break out of that cycle because they are unwilling to expend the energy that it takes for growth to occur. They never cross the mountain nor get to the river.

On the lower part of the continent, we are victims of circumstance: "I am the way I am because of my schooling, my parents or lack of luck." We are helplessly entangled in a world run by "others," always looking for someone to blame for our bad fortune and a savior in some form to rescue us. As long as you make someone else responsible for what you don't like in your life, you will always be looking for some external force to transform your experience and will be helpless to do so yourself.

You must cross that River of Blame. No one in your present or past has ever done anything to you and no one will ever save you. *You* chose all the experiences and circumstances of your past so you could become who you are.

Any transformation that occurs in your life *you* will also have to choose. As long as you blame someone for your experience, you will not be able to change it. *All the experiences in your life were sourced in your creative mind.*

Choose the past that you created, it's the raw clay you have to work with, and move up the path. A miraculous thing starts happening when you take responsibility for your experience. This is illustrated with two features on the Continent of Human Games. The House of *Healing* and the Field of *Rewards*.

When you have expended the energy to move past the River of Blame, a change starts to happen. The Caves of Pain are no longer your motivating force. It is the joy of life which now entices you to move along. What used to be effort, now becomes ease. Self-destructive habits fall away, your health improves, you meet people with positive attitudes toward life and, in general, there is a feeling of success and well-being in your life.

At this point, you move off the rocky path of perils and hard labor and onto the Road of Right Action. In India, it is called the path of *Dharma:* Walking in harmony. By this time, you have developed a sense of what's in alignment with your highest good and the highest good of all around you. If you stray, you will have a strong reaction that will bring you back into harmony with yourself and your environment.

Walking the Road of Right Action leads to the Garden of Sharing. This happens quite naturally while moving toward consciousness. We can no longer witness pain and suffering without wanting to assist in changing it. By sharing your path and the transformation it's brought, you can be a catalyst for the transformation of others.

When you arrive at the northern tip of the continent, you will discover the City of Personal Responsibility. In the city, you will experience living in a state of being continuously aware that you are creating your own life moment by moment. You will be able to rejoice in the ever-changing spectacle of form, color and feeling. You will witness the beauty and movement of the Infinite in physical form around and in you.

Our continent is surrounded by water. This water is a symbol for bliss. Bliss is the closest we can come to describing the state of being surrounding all the human games.

There are two aspects of life that are needed at every step on your journey. These are Choice and Risk. No growth will happen without you choosing it first. You must truly desire transformation and choose the state of being you want to experience. Then be willing to risk the old for the sake of the new. Whether it's moving out from the Caves of Pain or embarking at the City of Personal Responsibility for the Sea of Bliss, you should always be willing to take risks. Embrace risk-taking as a natural state in which to live; for on this path, life is never predictable. That's exactly what makes it so much fun to play on the Continent of Human Games.

3

EXPANDING
YOUR MIND

Imagine that you are a king ruling a very large territory. Since millions of people are affected by your decisions, you do not take your responsibilities lightly. In the spirit of wanting to do the best for your subjects, you conscientiously structure the routine of your day so that each important matter gets your fullest attention.

To prevent trivial intrusions from disturbing your focus, you shield yourself from the masses by creating a network of ministers, secretaries and under-secretaries to maintain order within your palace. You post a guard at the gate to minimize the comings and goings of unimportant traffic. Petty details are handled by underlings and are never even brought to you.

If an ordinary man wants to see you, first he must convince the gatekeeper that his business is urgent and of consequence. If he is successful in getting by your guard, a secretary will screen him to determine exactly what it is that needs attention. The secretary may refer this person to one of your ministers who will then make a determination as

27

to the significance of the matter and, in all probability, will make a promise to pass along the information.

When you are finally informed of the situation, if indeed it is ever deemed necessary that you be so informed, you are given a brief summary of the highlights contained in the message. It is not that you are rude, you simply must protect yourself from being constantly bombarded by people seeking audience with you. Your network for selectively screening would-be intruders allows you to serve everyone better.

The human brain actually works in a similar fashion. At any given moment, dozens of stimuli are bombarding your senses. If you were to give full attention to the sound of each raindrop falling, each car passing, plus the scents around you and the temperature of the air on your skin, obviously you would go into a state of overwhelm. Therefore, your brain is constructed in a way that allows you to focus on only certain details at any one time.

The mechanism that provides this function is known as the Reticular Activating System. The R.A.S. screens incoming data and only allows certain information to penetrate into your consciousness. For example, as you read these pages, your cat may walk past you and you might not even see it. Or if you live next to a train track, the R.A.S. may filter out the sound of trains passing every twenty minutes. Nothing reaches consciousness without first passing through the R.A.S. The R.A.S. is a filter like the network of guards and secretaries which protect a king from inconsequential intrusions.

As a result, you only see what your filters allow you to see. You only hear what your filters allow you to hear. This filtering mechanism is located in the base of the brain and is composed of electro-chemical impressions which are a memory bank of every experience you have ever had since you were born.

A graphic example of how this works can be found in a person who is afraid of spiders. Most phobias are born in a similar way. Suppose you are a baby who has never seen a spider. You are sitting on the floor of your room playing with your toys, when suddenly you notice a "big, black, crawly thing." Your R.A.S. has no prior experience of spiders and you reach out to investigate this new "toy." The spider crawls onto your hand and you giggle with delight. It walks up your arm and you gurgle with the pleasure of this gentle tickling sensation.

Now your mother enters the room. Your mother is terrified of spiders and when she sees her little baby on the floor with a giant spider, she emits a bloodcurdling scream, runs over to you, brushes the spider off your arm and squashes it with her shoe. She hugs you and caresses you and says something like, "Poor little baby, did that big, bad spider almost eat you up?"

Replay this same scene and look at what just happened inside the baby's brain. The R.A.S. first allowed the baby to totally relax and enjoy the spider because it had never been programmed to reject spiders. The brain is merely a biological computer. Its performance is a byproduct of how it has been programmed. When mother screams, the baby instantly reacts. All the baby's muscles tighten; the baby's heart accelerates and adrenalin is released into the infant's bloodstream. The entire chemistry of the tiny organism is instantly altered. This chemical change is recorded in the R.A.S. Since the brain is only a biochemical package of tissue which responds to electrical and chemical changes, it alters in response to the chemical change in the baby when mother screams.

This chemical reaction now becomes *programming*, a permanent part of the baby's filter system. The next time this baby sees a spider, the R.A.S. will automatically recall an "earlier similar" and will trigger the exact same body reaction that the baby had when its mother screamed. The heart will accelerate, all the muscles in the body will contract, adrenalin will enter the bloodstream and now we have a person who is afraid of spiders. People can be in their forties or fifties, having carried a phobia with them since infancy, and have absolutely no recollection of why they are afraid of spiders, or heights, or water or anything else.

All your habits, behaviors, phobias, blocks, neuroses, patterns, beliefs, goals and judgments were chemically programmed into you much like this baby was programmed about spiders. This programming is the filter through which you experience your life. It frequently distorts what is happening in the present by coloring a situation with unconscious memories from your past. We often "project" things onto events which alter our perception of what is really going on.

A dramatic example of how the R.A.S. can cripple us is the patient with hysterical blindness. In this instance, the eyes, nerves and brain are all physiologically perfect. The filtering mechanism, however, electro-chemically blocks visual images from consiousness. This illustration clearly demonstrates how powerful the Reticular Activating System really is. The R.A.S. literally determines what your experience of life will be.

The R.A.S. is entwined with a function often referred to as "ego." In this chapter, the words ego and R.A.S. are used interchangeably. The ego is a protection mechanism designed to serve you. However, when it is programmed in a certain way, it can actually have the effect of greatly hindering you. It is like a well-meaning person who might try to rescue someone after a car wreck, but because the good Samaritan is unaware of a broken spine, causes considerable injury.

Due to your programming and your ego, you may sometimes resemble a horse wearing blinders: able to see only a narrow strip of reality. Often, you may never even be seeing what is really going on; you may only be seeing what your ego "thinks" is going on.

All your automatic responses are a result of prior programming. To free yourself from this robot-like reaction to life, it is necessary to reprogram your bio-computer.

Reprogramming old limitations assists you in becoming more effective. Ego can be trained to serve you so that you can be master of it rather than ego mastering you. If you do not consciously examine your programming with the intention of reprogramming inappropriate responses, you will resemble a robot until the day you die. Consider the fish who bites the worm wrapped around a hook. In the struggle to escape, a corner of the fish's mouth may be ripped away. Days later, the fish again spots the bait and again bites. More of the fish's mouth is torn away. After accumulating enough horrible experiences with hooks, the fish may one day zoom up to the bait and suddenly stop, aware that there is a hook in that bait.

How often do you allow people and situations to bait *you?* How often are you going to keep repeating patterns before realizing that there is a hook in the bait? You may find yourself constantly arguing with your father over the same petty nonsense. The next time the subject comes up, why not close your mouth before biting the bait? Remember, there's a hook in it.

As you make a concerted effort to grow in self-awareness, you will become increasingly conscious of your conditioning or programming. At first, we tend to identify with our patterns, beliefs and behavior, thinking that this is who we are. The more you look within, however, the more you will begin to see that all this mental *activity* is just flowing around *you.* You wear it like a suit of clothes. Just like the suit creates your appearance, your programming also creates the illusion of being ''you.'' Yet we clearly see that there is a difference between us and our clothes. The clothes we wear can be changed and behind all ''that,'' here we are. The path of self-awareness teaches us to discriminate between what we really are and what we are not. Just like a suit, a dress or a pair of shoes, you can change your habits, remove your blocks and reprogram your behavior and beliefs.

When you first encounter a pattern or block which

doesn't serve you, you can do one of four things. One thing you can do is cry about it. You can blame people and circumstances, whine, curse and crumble in defeat. You can use it as a great excuse for not succeeding in life. You can rationalize why it's there and use it to elicit sympathy from others. All these things, of course, will not change it or cause it to go away.

The second thing you can do when encountering a phobia, pattern or belief which limits you is to talk about it. Some people carry their habits around as if they were conversation pieces. They seem to thrive on talking about their problems and failures. They often pay a therapist just so there will be someone to listen. Frequently, these people wind up trying to justify their behavior and shortcomings: "My mother was like that . . . and her mother also had this pattern." Their process of self-examination turns into "show and tell."

A third possibility is to pretend that everything is just fine. When introspection becomes too confrontive, some people simply try to ignore what they see. "I have no problems" becomes the response of someone who feels powerless to tackle the process of reprogramming ineffective and limiting habits. Arrogance and pride mask their inner sense of insecurity and they put considerable energy into trying to convince others that they are not only "normal," but even a bit better than most.

The fourth response, and the only one which results in change, is to simply examine whatever it is that you discover when you go through the procedure of looking within. If you are willing to objectively probe the tapes which have programmed your bio-computer, without identifying with them, in time you can change anything you discover which doesn't fully serve you. As soon as you can disassociate yourself from your "tapes" and realize that you are the "examiner" and not the activity or pattern being examined, that's how soon the process of reprogramming can take place.

Three simple methods that can effectively reprogram unwanted conditioning are covered in this book. Many of the more traditional methods are slow and often unsatisfactory. Frequently, people think that they are ''patients'' and give the responsibility for ''getting better'' to a doctor. The three methods about to be described depend solely upon *you* and no one else. Changing unwanted programming is a matter of taking personal responsibility for your growth. Don't worry about ''where'' the programming came from. Some ''therapies'' spend years trying to find out why someone got to be the way they are. If you were shot with a poison arrow, would you spend time asking, ''Where did this arrow come from? Was it shot from the North or the South? Who aimed it at me?'' If you have a poison arrow in your shoulder, you want to do only one thing: get it out!

You have the power to greatly expand your reality, eliminating what you don't want and manifesting what you do want. Einstein said we use only about a fifth of our brains. As you reprogram yourself, you will begin to expand. You no longer need to accept the limited reality that constant identification with your programming creates. Begin to know your true self as being vast and unlimited and see your patterns, personality and automatic responses as mere static on the infinite screen of your life.

THE THREE METHODS

Affirmations. The first method for reprogramming the ego is a simple process commonly known as *Affirmations.* An affirmation is a positive statement of what you want. It enables you to visualize the experience you desire as if you had already obtained it. There are several approaches to working with this technique and a later chapter will cover use of affirmations in detail.

Deliberate Emotional Intensity. The second method for reprogramming is called *Deliberate Emotional Intensity.* Whereas the power of affirmations lies in *frequency* of use, Deliberate Emotional Intensity relies on focusing emotions and concentrating intentions. Affirmations are written or repeated over and over until the desired pattern eventually replaces the unwanted one. It is a gentle approach toward getting the bio-computer to remember the new programming. It is entirely an internal process.

Deliberate Emotional Intensity is usually an external procedure. It takes one affirmation and blasts it into the bio-computer by screaming, fist pounding and sometimes tears. It is an extremely dynamic and powerful way of getting the mind to remember what it is you really want it to do. Before describing how to reprogram with Deliberate Emotional Intensity, let's look at its ultimate objective.

Suppose someone casually mentioned to you that their birthday was May first. After several years it would be quite natural for you to forget the date. However, if at the exact moment you were originally told that May first was this person's birthday a sudden explosion occurred and when you looked up three planes were skywriting "May First" in the heavens, it would make a lasting impression. If, in the same moment, a marching band appeared with a chorus singing "May First . . . May First," while a hundred belly dancers paraded around you with "May First" painted on their undulating stomachs and a thousand doves circled the area streaming banners imprinted "May First," chances are you would always remember the date.

Deliberate Emotional Intensity attempts to burn the desired affirmation into the brain so that it will never be forgotten. It requires a determined effort to be rid of the unwanted programming forever. Simply curl up on your bed and bury your face in a pillow; then scream the positive statement you want to program as loud as you can, over and over again until your entire body is affected by the intensity. Pounding the mattress also adds power to the process. The extreme emotional commitment involved often catalyzes tears. Crying further enhances the effectiveness of this method as more and more emotions come into play. A sample reprogramming phrase might be: "I love myself even when others reject me.''

The physical and emotional involvement create a change in body chemistry which passive writing of affirmations cannot produce as rapidly. This biochemical change in the body is recorded by electrical impulses surging through the R.A.S. If this procedure is sustained for enough time, perhaps even as long as an hour, it is possible to reprogram unwanted conditioning in just a few sessions. Recall the earlier description of the incident with the spider. That incident was recorded in the brain through electro-chemical alterations of the brain's usual equilibrium. By again altering the electro-chemical balance of the bio-computer during reprogramming, one tape can be replaced by another.

Direct Experience. The third method for reprogramming the R.A.S. is by substituting a direct powerful experience which is so intense that it literally overshadows the earlier experience which resulted in the unwanted programming. For example, firewalking is more and more becoming a widely practiced occurrence and is included in many growth seminars. If all your life you held a belief that you would burn your feet by walking on glowing, red coals and then you participated in a firewalk where you walked on coals exceeding 1200°F. without burning your feet, you would never again be able to return to your old belief.

Similarly, the entire world once believed that the earth was flat. However, once it was demonstrated that the earth was round, never again could we go back to the old belief. When something you have always believed to be true is *experienced* to be false, or something you believed false is *experienced* to be true, your programming about that is permanently changed.

An ancient tale refers to a pickpocket who encountered a saint. He never even really saw the saint; all he saw was the man's pocket. If you do not reprogram yourself, you too will go through life missing all there is to experience, being constantly forced to see only what your programming allows you to see. It's like having tunnel vision; you'll tend to constantly see only what you fear and what you desire. By taking the time and energy to reprogram, you can become like the saint who when meeting a pickpocket sees only the man's soul.

4

SEVEN
LIFE REQUIREMENTS

If your life ever seems stressful, unexciting or limited, it is an indication that something vital is missing and that you've allowed yourself to stop growing. This chapter provides a simple framework for examining yourself in a way that can reveal the "missing ingredient."

There are basically *Seven Life Requirements*, seven things that we need if we wish to feel completely fulfilled as human beings. Sometimes we move so fast traveling through life that even though we sense "something" may be "off," we never really know what it is. However, at any moment, you can stop, look within and ask, "What is it that I should be doing right now?" If you pause long enough to ask the question, there will be an answer. The usual answer is that you have overlooked one of seven critical requirements to obtain the most out of living.

SEVEN LIFE REQUIREMENTS

1. Financial Security
2. Good Feelings
3. Self-worth
4. Active Compassion
5. Creative Expression
6. Attentive Awareness
7. Constant Connectedness

1. Financial Security. It's impossible to grow and be happy if your basic security needs aren't being met. Security means food, clothes and shelter. In today's society, these three things are equivalent to money. Money is a basic means of exchange which enables us to secure edibles, wearing apparel and a home. If we do not have these three things, it is hard to be happy. It is difficult to encourage someone to seek God-consciousness if they don't know from where their next meal will come.

Of course, in our youth these needs are provided by parents, or if one is handicapped, they may be provided by an institution. However, most of us depend on a source of monitary income so that we can at least take care of ourselves. Before looking any further for happiness, examine your ability to provide yourself with basic sustenance.

2. Good Feelings. The second thing you need as a human being is regular good feelings. These can be provided by hiking, attending theatre, sex, food, meditation, music, loving relationships or almost any sensation you find pleasant. Each morning you should be able to wake up and feel that life is good and worth living another day. Often we hear about people who have plenty of money and yet wind up killing themselves. Obviously then, money alone cannot bring happiness. Day-to-day living should *feel* good—it is a basic Life Requirement.

If regular good feelings are missing from your life, you are going to have an experience that life is just not working.

This can be illustrated by a situation that actually happened in New York. Hilda Charlton, a spiritual teacher in Manhattan, was approached after class by a young man who told her he was going to go home and kill himself.

"Why are you telling me this?" she asked.

"I was hoping you would somehow know how to stop me from doing it," he replied.

"If I tell you to do something, will you promise to do it?" Hilda responded.

"Sure."

So Hilda told the fellow to stop by a grocery store on the way home and buy a chocolate cake mix, as well as all the specified ingredients. She instructed him to go home, bake the cake, allow it to cool a bit, eat a large slice and then phone her immediately.

Later that evening the phone rang. "Hello, Hilda, I just finished eating the cake."

"How do you feel?" she asked.

"Great. I don't know what got into me, but I'm fine now."

An ancient truth is, "This too shall pass." Sometimes it's just the absence of good feelings that brings about depression. Can you imagine anyone killing himself when he's feeling good? Don't underestimate the value of regular good feelings; they are a basic requirement of life. *Don't deny yourself pleasure because you have some idea that it is decadent or unspiritual.* Quite the contrary. It is a necessary part of growth. If you ever feel "down," go to a funny movie or buy yourself a new shirt. Love yourself enough to do something nice for yourself.

3. Self-worth. Self-worth means that you feel good about yourself, you respect yourself, you feel worthy of success, have a sense that you are powerful enough to control your own destiny and you feel okay about yourself even when other people put you down. Don't be confused by your impressions of people with "superiority complexes." There really is no such thing as a superiority complex. People who always seek to build themselves up or subtly put others down do so because they actually are suffering from an "inferiority complex."

Self-worth means knowing that you are PERFECT *just the way you are* and accepting yourself completely. You let go of guilt and stop regretting anything which is now past. You know yourself to be a genuine expression of the Universe, an aspect of the perfection which exists naturally *everywhere* in the cosmos. Can you possibly deny that the Universe is perfect, *just the way it is?* You certainly can't point at the night sky and say, "The Universe is *almost* perfect, but that star is in the wrong place." You are a part of the perfect Universe, just like any star, tree, stone or turtle.

This point can be illustrated quite humorously. Imagine you are a housewife. While cooking the evening meal you become distracted by a phone call and everything you prepared is burned to a crisp. Your husband comes home and attacks you with insults. "You are hopeless," he bellows, "you can't even boil water without burning it!"

If you don't have a sense of self-worth, you become intimidated by your husband's outburst and immediately go into feelings of unworthiness. You forget who you really are. You suddenly believe that you are a far cry from being perfect.

Well, if such were the case, then obviously the community you live in could not be perfect, because when something is perfect, then every dimension of it must, of course, be perfect. A blemish on any portion of something mars its total perfection. So now we must also deny the perfection of the continent on which you live. That continent is a part of the earth, so the planet earth can no longer be regarded as perfect. If we want to be completely accurate with our perspective, we have to say that the solar system of planets revolving around the sun is obviously not perfect; because it, too, includes YOU. The sun is only one of billions of stars in our galaxy known as the Milky Way, and now we have to label the entire galaxy as imperfect. In fact, this galaxy represents only a tiny fraction of all the galaxies that comprise the

Universe; so it is easy to see that the Universe can't possibly be perfect, because woven into the cosmic fabric ... there *you* are.

When seen from this angle, it becomes ludicrous to see yourself as ever being less than perfect. The Universe *IS* perfect just the way it is and it includes *you* ... in fact, right now, it wouldn't be the same *without* you.

No matter who you are and no matter what you do, you can know your self-worth because you are in fact PERFECT ... right now! Never forget that regardless of your actions or other people's judgments of you, your perfection remains unchanged.

It is important to forgive yourself for anything you have done in the past. The past is gone and exists only in your mind. *Each day you are born anew and guilt can never make a positive contribution to your life or anyone else's.* God is not a huge meat axe in the sky, poised over your neck waiting to decapitate you for all your sins. Everyone makes mistakes on their path of finding themselves. If you regret something you said or did, notice that you may have behaved inappropriately, learn the lesson you need to learn and resolve to act more appropriately next time. You are perfect even making mistakes.

So far, we have covered the first three of seven basic human Life Requirements. We must have our security needs met, we have to supply ourselves with regular good feelings, and we need a sense of self-worth. Let's compare these human needs with those of a dog. In a sense, dogs also have these needs. However, have you ever known a dog to worry about them, have anxiety attacks or lie awake fearing that its master may soon take a vacation and forget to leave food? A dog always feels secure. As humans, we not only fret over our real security needs, we also create others that don't exist.

Sometimes humans behave as if they need approval in order to survive. If someone disapproves of us, we frequently react as if our very survival is being threatened. Dogs don't do that. Dogs don't get bored either. Can you imagine some hound thinking that there aren't enough good feelings around and contemplating suicide? Do you suppose dogs experience lingering unworthiness? You can look a dog in the eye and say, "BAD! BAD! BAD!," without it losing so much as one night's sleep. Dogs feel perfectly all right in their "dogness." Canines have an easy time being canines. They spend little energy focusing on these first three aspects of life and yet they appear quite happy and content. Actually, the first three things we've been discussing are quite easy to attain. Yet most people go through life struggling with just these; trying to make it to a place where they can experience feeling the same fulfillment as any dog.

These first three Life Requirements are basic. We have them in common with every other mammal walking the earth. Now, let's examine the four aspects of life which are uniquely human.

4. Active Compassion. Compassion is an expression of love and charity. It is not just "loving feelings," but a dynamic activity. If what you call love is not reflected in service to others, then what you are experiencing is really only *Good Feelings.*

Real love is something which flows out and effects others. This type of love is a distinct human quality. You actually possess the ability to love *unconditionally.* Jesus told his followers to love their enemies, because if they only loved those who were nice to them, they were no different from anyone else. This quality of love means that you can serve and accept *everyone* unconditionally—*including yourself.*

The love now being described doesn't even have to be directed at people. You can express it by simply going out and picking litter off the street. This kind of love is an incredible medicine; you can practice it anywhere and at anytime and it will always have the effect of making you feel good. Service to others is an excellent remedy you can give yourself if ever you feel depressed.

There is no limit to how you can serve. You can tithe or be a volunteer; by visiting an elderly shut-in or reading to a blind neighbor you can create goodness in your own life, as well as theirs. *Giving* in this way is really *receiving*. It appears as if you are serving someone else, but the truth of it is that *they are serving you* by allowing you to serve them. This quality of love is very different from just having loving feelings which remain unexpressed. The distinction is made clear in the story of a fellow who was addicted to constantly immersing himself in pleasurable sensations. On his wall he had numerous pictures of nude women and every evening he would come home, smoke pot and watch porno movies. His bookcase was cluttered with bottles of alcohol and *Playboy* magazines.

Finally, a friend of his who had just returned from India chided him on his amoral and hedonistic lifestyle. On an impulse, the fellow responded by taking a trip to India himself. The excursion actually had the effect of touching him deeply and he returned home believing himself to be a changed man.

Immediately he removed the alcohol, drugs and pornography from his life and redecorated his room. Now his walls were postered with pictures of Krishna, Rama, Buddha, Jesus and other saints. In place of his porno collection, he built a small altar with candles and incense. Instead of his old habits, he now spent his evenings chanting sacred *mantras*.

"I have really transformed," the fellow thought. "I have become so spiritual and loving."

Nonsense! He is right back in *Good Feelings*. All he did was exchange one set of pleasurable sensations for another collection of sensations. He is finally pointed in the right direction, but until he goes out into the world and does something for another person and uses all this new energy to improve the quality of someone else's life, until he expresses what he is experiencing internally by outflowing it in the form of service, it is not the love we call *Active Compassion*. It is still *Good Feelings*.

Some people manage to effortlessly accumulate the first three necessary ingredients of life. They have ample wealth, considerable amounts of pleasurable stimulation and a strong degree of self-worth. However, if they do not have a deep, meaningful sense of what love is, everything else seems hollow. As poets have often said: Love is something that if you don't have it, it doesn't matter what else you have.

Yet, without the underlying foundation of the first three necessities, love may occasionally shimmer across your horizon; but then it's gone. To be in a position to effectively serve, you must first securely *anchor yourself* so that you have the strength to offer support to others.

5. Creative Expression. The fifth Life Requirement is very subtle. Even when the first four have been attained and a person is basically happy, days can sometimes appear flat and without sparkle. *Creative Expression* is like perfume or seasoning added to something which already is in itself pretty satisfying. When it is absent, we sometimes feel frustrated for no apparent reason.

If you are seeking nothing less than complete fulfillment, you must have a way of expressing yourself. The possibilities here are almost endless: a hobby, cooking, writing, teaching, sports, and so on and so forth.

It should be noted here that all the previously mentioned Life Requirements can overlap. The way in which you earn your livelihood can provide you with good feelings and self-respect. It can also be a service and give you an opportunity to express yourself creatively; an example being actors or actresses who perform in consciousness-raising showcases that tour the world alerting people to the hazards of nuclear waste. At once, all five categories we've mentioned are simultaneously covered. Another example could be the seamstress who gets paid while also expressing herself creatively.

All these things can intertwine, or they can exist independently from each other. If you are feeling anxious, grievous, blocked, depressed or bored, carefully examine your life and see what's missing. Are you serving in some way? Are you expressing your creativity? There can be no doubt that if you are fulfilled in each of the first five Life Requirements, you will be a very happy person. Being happy is not difficult; it's actually quite easy once you learn how to do it. Yet being happy is not the ultimate goal of being alive. there is a spiritual dimension to life that lies beyond happiness. The sixth and seventh Life Requirements are specifically concerned with the subject of spirituality.

6. Attentive Awareness. Paying attention was introduced earlier as one of *Five Points of Power* and will be discussed again later. It is a critically important aspect of developing self-awareness and spirituality. It represents an entirely new way of "seeing." *Attentive Awareness* enables us to be completely united with our experience at any given moment. When you eat—pay attention! When washing dishes—pay attention! While on the toilet—pay attention!

Attentive Awareness eventually gives birth to the spiritual quality of "non-attachment," the primary focus of Buddha's teaching. Once non-attachment arises within you, everything and anything becomes acceptable. It no longer matters what it is that you are actually paying attention to. Suddenly *everything* seems pleasurable or causes further growth.

Even pain can become a spiritual experience at this level. Although animals can be aware of pain, it is only humans who can be aware that they are aware of pain. By continually paying attention, you will begin to disassociate yourself from the melodrama you are constantly witnessing on the movie screen of your life and you will experience yourself as "the watcher." In this way, you can welcome *each and every* experience as it arises. You no longer need to grasp after "this" and push away "that."

You can learn from every life situation without reacting. *Attentive Awareness* brings you beyond judgmentalness: nothing is "good" or "bad"—everything just "is." A simple tale describes a man who demonstrated this state quite well.

There was a poor man whose only horse ran away. When his neighbor sighed, "Oh how unfortunate you are," the man replied, "Maybe." The next day the stallion returned leading an entire herd of wild horses into the man's corral. As he closed the gate, his neighbor appeared shouting jubilantly,

"Oh, how lucky you are." The man's only reply was, "Maybe." Several days later, the man's son attempted to break one of the new horses and badly fractured his leg in the process. When the neighbor lamented, "Such a tragedy," again the man's only reply was, "Maybe." Shortly thereafter a war broke out and soldiers canvassed the rural farms drafting young men into the king's army. Of course, because of his broken leg, the boy was exempted. "How fortunate," exclaimed the neighbor. The man replied, "Maybe."

The spiritual awareness and non-attachment this man shows is born of "watching." It transmutes life into a constantly active process of meditation. It would be impossible to ever again be lonely once you become self-aware. You will "sense" a spiritual presence that is constantly with you and within you . . . always watching . . . aware of everything you are aware of. The watcher sees what you see, hears what you hear, smells what you smell, experiences whatever you experience. A whole new dimension unfolds as a result of cultivating *Attentive Awareness*.

Again it is important to note that these areas of growth are not necessarily neatly ordered and in progressive succession. It is possible to spend one day experiencing *Active Compassion* and yet wake up the next morning worrying about bills. By paying attention, you can in any given moment observe where you are *in that moment*. You can also be aware that you are aware.

As you evolve, you will constantly move about and between all these aspects of consciousness. When you are grieving over the loss of a favorite pleasure, you can observe yourself dancing in the realm of needing a *Good Feeling*. When you find yourself snatching poetry from the air, note that *Creative Expression* is upon you. Never think of one quality as being "better" or "worse" than another. They all move around us and we around them in an endless ballet. Such is the way Spiritual Reality develops.

   7. **Constant Connectedness.** After you have spent some time paying attention, an amazing thing will happen: You

will start experiencing more and more frequently that you are *constantly* connected to the whole Cosmos. You *are* always *connected* to the earth, the solar system, the stars, the Universe. You are, in fact, connected to everything that exists. As humans, we possess the potential to realize our connection to *ALL THAT IS,* which many refer to simply as God. *You are a part of that!*

We frequently hear, "we are one," sung in songs and written in books. What does that mean? It means there is only one unified energy everywhere. *You* are a part of *that!* All the power of the Universe is at your disposal. People who have realized this have actually been able to heal themselves of cancer. Once they feel all the power of the Universe surging inside them—*right now!*—they are able to literally rearrange their atoms with visualization. They own the power that comes from *knowing* that they are connected to the source of creation.

In India, Swami Sathya Sai Baba creates material objects out of air. Is he violating the laws of the Universe? No. It is just that we don't yet understand all the laws of the Universe. He says to people, "I am God. You are also God. The only difference between you and me is that I *know* I'm God."

It is possible for us to realize that *everything* is God, including ourselves. We need not ever die once we know who we *really* are. When we realize that we are God, every resource in the Universe is at our command and disposal. You are never alone; you are never separate. The realization of this transforms your entire reality. When you continually experience that you are a part of the Universe and are *never* disconnected, you have attained what Easterners term "Enlightenment."

These *Seven Life Requirements* correspond to the seven *chakras* described in ancient Sanskrit scriptures. They also parallel Maslow's Seven Centers of Consciousness. Knowledge of them can serve to guide you on your path of self-development. One is not any "better" than the others and you should never punish yourself for not being in one area as opposed to another. Never compare your evolution with someone else's. After all, in grammar school, doesn't every seventh grader have to attend all the grades before the seventh?

Consider also the rockets we send to the moon. They are actually always off course. The computers are constantly correcting to the right, then to the left, and as a result of the self-correcting guidance system, the rocket eventually lands on target. By examining yourself on a regular basis, you can grow using these seven points as a guide.

A good thought to remember as we close this chapter is the observation: "Every journey of a thousand miles always begins by just taking one step."

The next time you feel frustrated or unfulfilled, reflect on these Seven Life Requirements and see where your life is incomplete. The chapters which follow will offer you methods for providing yourself with everything you need.

5

SETTING INTENTIONS

Our mind is like a movie projector, life being the screen on which the mental movies take on form and dimension. All our beliefs, ideas and programming become reality as they are projected onto the screen of life, to be experienced by us, the projector of the movie. Have you ever wondered what's in your mind? Take a look at your life. It will be a clear mirror of the beliefs you hold about yourself and life.

Do you have enough money? Does success come easily? Do you have friends with whom you can joyously share the adventure of living? Every external effect in your life is there as a result of a mental image you hold. That mental picture has been projected out and now exists in three-dimensional form to be experienced by you. Frequently, during childhood you absorb your parents' images of life and then find yourself repeating *their* patterns.

Take the man, for example, who after a few disastrous relationships, has finally found the perfect mate. She is so unlike anyone he has ever experienced. She is intelligent and yet sweet, capable and yet devoted. Three months down the road, however, we catch him saying: "You burn the toast just like my mother." Not only that, but she walks like his mother, talks like his mother and insists he make his bed, just like his mother! This poor woman had never burned toast before in her life and could not have cared less about beds being made. What's happening? She is responding to his mental movies and all of a sudden, he has the repetition of previous relationships, and along with that, burnt toast.

Of course, the woman's inner movies will nicely harmonize with her mate's, for *her mother* also burned toast. So here we have another relationship teetering on the edge of disaster over burnt toast.

If you don't like the movie being played, don't attack the movie screen, change the reel! There is no sense in trying to change the external in order to transform your experience. Another new relationship, a third car, this time a sportscar, or another baby won't create satisfaction; because in a few months, you'll be back to "burnt toast." The old patterns will repeat themselves.

Realize that every external effect is the result of internal programming. Change that programming if you want your life to take on a new form. The energy that can bring about that change is called *intention*. Using the analogy of the movie projector again, *intention* is the light that shines through a particular frame and projects it brilliantly onto the screen. All you have to do is select the movie and turn on the light and it will be projected on the screen. The brighter the light, the more vivid the movie. The more clear you are with your intention, the quicker and more accurately your desires will manifest.

This next illustration was originally developed for children. It is such an effective teaching tool that it is now used for adults as well.

Jasper lives in a house near the woods. He has a favorite spot where he meditates in those woods. He awakens one morning with the desire to meditate there. Along with that desire, he gets a picture in his mind of his special place. *All thoughts have mental pictures attached to them. When you choose to act as a result of those pictures, you have set an intention.* Jasper feels good when he looks at his picture, so he packs his things and heads for the woods. *The strength of the feelings associated with the picture will determine the strength of your intention.*

Just as he is about to enter the woods, he encounters an enormous field of thistles. Jasper's path is blocked by plants that scratch and prick. *Often when wanting to manifest an intention, you will encounter obstacles or barriers.* At first he is discouraged: "Maybe I'll just go home. I guess I'm not supposed to meditate." Then the mental picture of his special place in the woods comes to mind and warm feelings flood his body.

He gets inspired: "I could buy a goat and let her eat the thistles. I could pogo stick through them. I could get my stilts and walk high above them!" *When your intentions or mental images have enough energy associated with them, they will inspire you to find creative ways to overcome obstacles.*

Jasper hurries home to get his rubber boots and sickle. By swinging the sickle and chopping down the thistles he clears himself a path. Jasper then continues merrily on his way.

As he is crossing a little bridge, his eye is caught by silvery shapes moving in and out of the blue-green shadows in the water below him. Jasper used to love fishing and fond memories flood his mind. There are now two pictures battling for his attention: one of that special place to meditate, the other of fishing. *The picture that has more energy will be the one that manifests.*

Let's leave Jasper standing on the bridge for a moment. It was said earlier in this chapter, our mental images are responsible for the experiences in our lives. If you are wanting a new job and are excited about the possibilities of higher pay and greater challenges, you will have positive mental images of getting that job as you go for your interview. But, if along with that, you have a terror of interviews plus a lot of negative memories of rejections from the past, you will be in Jasper's position exactly. Two possibilities are battling for the upper hand. Here is where the picture that has more energy associated with it ends up being manifested. If your fear of being rejected is stronger than your excitement about the job, you *will* be rejected.

As Jasper stands on the bridge, he remembers the dancing columns of sunlight coming through the trees by his favorite place and warm feelings spread through his body. He leaves the bridge and thoughts of fishing behind as he continues toward his special spot.

Suddenly, there is a fork in Jasper's path. One way leads into the forest, the other to a distant mountain gleaming in the sunlight. Again, temptation strikes him. Jasper has heard so much about that mountain. Would it be wrong if he chose to change direction and head for the mountain? Of course not; but he must let go of desires for his special spot if he chooses to do that. Otherwise, those desires will be a continual distraction on the mountain.

To digress, a wonderful *Zen* story illustrates this point. Two monks meet on the road. After their formal bows, one asks the other, "Where are you going tonight, brother?" The other replies, "To the temple to pray. Where are you going this fine evening?" The first monk responds, "I am on my way to the house of pleasure for a night with the ladies."

They bow to each other and both continue on their way. That night, in the house of pleasure, there is a very distressed monk. All he can think about is his brother monk praying. Yet, in the temple, is the other monk any more relaxed? No! All that's on his mind is his brother in the house of pleasure. This illustrates the importance of completely accepting the choices you make and surrendering to the experiences that go along with them.

Returning to Jasper, we find him experiencing a flood of good feelings as he realizes that what he wants more than anything else is to be under his tree in the woods. *When you have difficult choices to make, your body will usually advise you of the better choice by flooding you with good feelings in connection with the appropriate picture.* It takes Jasper only a short time before he is contentedly nestled at the roots of the tall trees in that special spot that he held in his mind. *Any intention on which you continually focus energy will become a reality.*

When setting intentions, choose your desired goal. Then start building the energy behind that intention by seeing all the details of the picture. Experience the satisfaction you're going to feel, the joy you'll experience and all the rewards of attaining your goal. *Experience it as if it's already happened.* Realize that there is nothing that can stop it from manifesting. Then let go of it, knowing that you've planted a seed and it will grow.

As you do this experiential visualization, you might find your fears and doubts creeping in. Don't try to push them out of the way because you are afraid to give them power. Watch them and acknowledge them, as if they were an old over-cautious aunt who really wants your good, but whose advice seems to be restricting you. Allow them to go *through* you without influencing you. Then go back to visualizing your intention, knowing that nothing can stop it from manifesting. Remember, it's the pictures you hold in your mind and focus energy on that become the reality you live in.

The act of setting intentions can bring about a positive shift in your experience of living. It gives your mind a direction on which to focus and a scale by which to measure your progress. Without intentions, you are like a rudderless ship, hoping that the currents of life will bring you to fulfilling experiences. If you want to guarantee your growth, set intentions and begin manifesting the transformation you desire.

You might want to start giving yourself direction right now by *listing* your intentions. What is your intention for the next week, month and year? Write down any positive action you can take to realize your intentions. For each of the following subjects, list your *final goal*. Create an intention regarding: your *health* and *body*, including diet; *money* and physical objects (i.e., car, house, etc.); *relationships*, both old and new;

sexuality (why live with sexual discomfort when you can transform your experience by setting an intention to do so?); self-destructive *habits; personality* and self-worth; areas of creative *self-expression; spiritual evolution.*

Of course, there are many other areas in which you might want to set intentions. Remember that an intention is a seed being planted by your conscious mind in your subconscious. It's like the farmer planting his seed in the earth, leaving it there and then going on to other things, knowing that the rains will cause it to grow. Your conscious mind can now go on to other things, confident that the subconscious will nourish your intentions and bring them into reality.

Frequently, people have difficulty attaining what they believe is the purpose of their lives. However, there really is only one purpose to life: to feel fulfilled and in harmony with the world around you. Different people experience fulfillment from different things. Whatever you seek, obviously it is meant to bring you to the same point of satisfaction that others desire to attain, though perhaps via a different route.

If you are experiencing difficulty attaining your goals, it could be that you are not focusing your energy. Here is a simple exercise that will help you achieve oneness of purpose by revealing what your true priorities are *at this time.* After all, if you waste time and energy on things that are *off purpose,* you will delay or prevent yourself from ever succeeding.

Cut some paper into twenty-five small pieces measuring about two inches square. On five pieces, write down the five most valuable *relationships* in your life. Then, on another five pieces, write five plans you have for the *future.* Now write five material *possessions* you are attached to. Next, write five aspects of your *lifestyle* which you consider important. Finally, on the five remaining pieces, write five things you like about your own *character.*

Lay the twenty-five pieces of paper on a table in front of you so they can all be seen. Then, *quickly* and without thinking, count out loud—one, two, three—and grab three pieces of paper. Instantly crumple them and throw them to the floor.

Again count out loud—one, two, three—and snatch three more pieces of paper, crumple them and toss them to the floor. Continue this procedure until four pieces of paper remain. Your subconscious will thus have revealed your four most important priorities at this moment. Honor these things by giving them your primary focus time-wise, and you will certainly feel more fulfilled.

6

AFFIRMATIONS

As you grow in consciousness, you will start noticing how thoughts that reflect your beliefs and programming run through your mind coloring your experience. In truth, these thoughts not only influence your experience, but actually *create* it. An affirmation is a positive thought or statement which you can use to counteract a belief that no longer supports you. It can help create any experience you desire.

Affirmations are used in several ways. Writing is the most common approach to ingrain a new thought in the mind. The positive statement you desire to create as reality should be written over and over again in the same form. It's also beneficial to include your first name. For example: "I, Jane, am loved." Since so much of your programming was received from an external source, the pronouns can also be changed: "She, Jane, is loved," "You, Jane, are loved." This simple statement would be written for approximately five minutes.

It's important that you write with full concentration, noting when your mind skips into thoughts about unpaid bills or that cup of coffee you left on the counter. When writing affirmations, you are gently reprogramming your mind. Sometimes you will be challenging beliefs that might have survival energy attached to them. There is a good chance that you may often find yourself in resistance. Just note the discomfort you are generating. Don't let yourself be distracted, but continue to write until your mind is quiet and your body is again relaxed.

This can be repeated twice daily. The best times seem to be upon waking and before going to sleep. It doesn't matter how often you write your affirmations; but obviously the more energy you expend, the sooner you will have results.

It's best to only work with two or three affirmations at one sitting. Keep them simple, to the point and always write them in the positive form. "I am no longer afraid of heights," is a negation of a negative and will not be effective. The picture the mind creates with that statement is fear of heights. To turn it into an effective affirmative, you would word it: "I, Tom, feel relaxed and at peace in high places."

Allow yourself to enjoy the process of transformation. Be playful. Write affirmations on little cards and stick them to the mirror in your bathroom, your refrigerator, the dashboard of your car. Sing them to yourself as you wash your face or shave in the morning. As you find yourself attaining the goals set by your affirmations, reward yourself: take yourself out to dinner or buy yourself some flowers. Become your own best playmate on your journey of self-discovery. Let your inner voice become a loving friend who encourages you, rather than a disapproving parent.

Affirmations can also be taped so you can listen to them while driving the car or doing housework. Be creative with this process. *Pay attention* to your thoughts; catch the ways in which you put yourself down and change your internal messages to supportive statements. You deserve all the love you can give yourself.

Resentment will often stop progress when writing affirmations. Forgiveness is one of the most powerful tools on this path. To forgive someone doesn't mean that they were right and you were wrong. It is simply disconnectig yourself from the incident that caused you distress. *If you find a past situation always coming to mind, it may be calling for forgiveness.* Make a list of all the people and occurrences you are now willing to forgive. Make a second list of the people from whom you desire forgiveness. Never let these lists get old, but keep adding to them as more memories are stimulated.

Sometimes our negative program or our attachment to a certain belief is so strong that it will hinder us from producing a desired result. If you find yourself writing affirmations on a certain subject with no change occurring after a considerable length of time, it may be that you need to cleanse yourself of attachments to your past.

This can be done by forgiving people who reinforced the negative program or by a simple visualization. See yourself connected by invisible cords to all the events and people from the past that have had any relationship with the program you are wanting to eliminate. Then gently, one by one, disconnect those cords. This will leave you feeling cleansed and free to reprogram with affirmations.

An affirmation should always be written as if the goal has already been attained. "I *am* lovable," "I *am* self-confident." Along with writing the affirmation in present time, *visualize* the result as if it had already arrived. *See* it vividly, in brilliant color. *Experience* the feelings you will have when this comes to pass. Make it as real as possible.

Set your goals high, knowing that life is a mirror of your beliefs and attitudes. As your beliefs start shifting, you will easily attain things you once believed impossible. Miracles are not only possible, they are part of your birthright as a human being.

Now is the time for you to take hold of the ship's rudder and take control of your life. What is it you are wanting? Nothing will stop you if you are willing to use the tools given here. You are meant to manifest God's glory on earth, so give yourself all the beauty that's possible to experience.

Your joy will ripple out and touch others. Start transforming the world you live in now.

The following list is a good introduction to affirmations. Read it through slowly. The affirmations you react to most strongly will be the ones you need to work with. After reading the affirmations listed here, begin composing your own.

- I am lovable.
- It's safe to be loved.
- I love being alive.
- The more I enjoy life, the better life gets.
- I think highly of myself in the presence of others.
- I am good enough.
- I am successful.
- I am intelligent.
- I always give myself what I need.
- All my relationships are successful.
- People want me to win.
- I am self-confident.
- I express myself well.
- I am abundant.
- I make money easily.
- My body mirrors my inner beauty.
- My body vibrates with health and vitality.
- I am strong and joyfully alive.
- The more beauty I see in others, the more beautiful I become.

7

INVISIBLE GUIDANCE

Meditation serves many purposes and has many forms. It relaxes the body and mind, stimulates a flow of spiritual energy, resolves unanswered questions, promotes health and longevity, and brings us in contact with our own inner guidance. Meditation can be watching thoughts or breath, emptying the mind, focusing on an external object, sitting or walking. In all forms, it connects us to Eternal Wisdom. Once this connection is established, the entire process of living becomes noticeably easier.

Any of several techniques can assist you in your discovery of invisible guidance. What works for one person may not suit another. It is an extremely personal thing which each individual must experiment with until he or she feels a comfortable and dependable connection with his or her own guidance.

There is a story about a ship's captain which serves to remind us of how inner guidance can work. A large ocean liner was passing through a narrow straight congested with large, sharp rocks. The captain was an experienced old salt who had sailed for many years. Suddenly, one of the new young officers on the bridge shouted, "Captain, if you continue going full steam ahead, we're going to hit those rocks."

The captain was outraged at the very idea that a new, inexperienced tenderfoot dared to challenge his abilities. He reached for the horn and shouted to his engineer, "Full steam ahead . . . *sideways!*" The ship, of course, got scuttled on the rocks.

In this illustration, the captain represents the ego. The young officer represents inner guidance. If you think back over your life, you will probably notice that every time you have ever made a mistake which had disastrous results, there was a small, soft voice within you advising you not to proceed. By ingoring that guidance, you yourself created the unwanted results. Ego's voice is so loud it often drowns out the quieter voice of guidance. Meticulous skill must be developed if you are to discern between the conflicting inner voices you hear so that you don't constantly wind up going "full steam ahead sideways."

One technique that can assist you in distinguishing between conflicting inner voices and contacting your true guide is commonly known as a pendulum. Pendulums are used in various ways, but the way we are about to describe is the most simple. It can be made by attaching any weight, especially a ring, to a cord or thread about a half-meter in length. When you hold the unweighted end of the thread in your hand, the free swinging motion of the pendulum resembles the movable arm of a seismograph that visually shows even the tiniest tremor in the earth below.

By holding the pendulum in front of you, it becomes a bio-feedback device that indicates what is happening inside you on a very subtle level. It works like this. Sit quietly and focus on the question or course of action that is causing you to be indecisive. Try to formulate an "either/or" image of the situation. A question that can be answered "Yes" or "No" is ideal. When the question has crystallized in your mind, pick up the pendulum. Ask aloud, "What is the sign for *Yes?*" Hold the pendulum steady in one hand as you keep asking for the sign which indicates *"Yes."*

Eventually, the pendulum will begin to move. It may swing in an arc from North to South or from East to West. It may turn in a circular motion. Regardless of how it moves, note that this movement represents *"Yes."* Now repeat the process to obtain a sign for *"No."*

Once signs for *Yes* and *No* are obtained, sit quietly and hold the pendulum while repeating your question aloud. Keep repeating the question until the pendulum moves. It may take a while until it does move, but eventually it will move. What is being revealed is your body's response to the still, quiet voice within; the one which best knows the appropriate action in any given instance.

The pendulum is not a mystical, esoteric trinket, but a simple bio-feedback device that allows you to tune-in to your own inner feelings. Though it may appear bizarre to an uneducated onlooker if they suddenly walked in while you were using it, a pendulum is neither an occult nor psychic procedure. It is a sound, scientific and reliable instrument for discovering information you already possess, but are having difficulty retrieving.

Always work with the pendulum in a quiet, calm area. Use it several times so as to confirm its accuracy. Initially, you may use the pendulum in a mood of faith, but after continued use you will see how accurate it is and your faith will eventually evolve into trust.

Your existence on earth is a byproduct of love. You were conceived in an act of lovemaking and all great religions teach that it is out of supreme love that the Lord created us. Certainly anything created in the spirit of love is cared for and watched over. Therefore, it is natural for you to want contact with this force which can care for you and guide you safely down the path. *The inner voice is that care and guidance.* Too often, though, the blustery voice of the ego drowns out the more subtle whisperings. Even when you hear the whisper, sometimes you may pretend you don't or choose to ignore it, proceeding "full steam ahead—sideways."

It is essential for you to pause periodically and assess your position. Are you aligned with the goals you've set? Are you causing anyone injury or harm by your actions? Are you involved in any self-destructive patterns or habits? Regardless of where you are going in life, it is wise to at least know where you are right now. Within each of us is that "small voice" which can accurately tell us exactly where things are at. It is natural to doubt the validity of invisible guidance when you first experiment with it, but after forming a relationship with it, you will find that doubt soon evaporates.

Your inner guide is your only true teacher. Whenever you think you are learning something new, what is really happening is that your inner sense is merely recognizing something that had always been known to you on a very deep inner level. Sometimes, external teachings are needed to stimulate the internal connection that allows your own perfect wisdom to flow.

Another way to contact inner guidance can be by *asking for what you want*. In a meditative or prayerful way, you can verbalize your need for guidance by pretending that the Source of Creation, the Great Mystery, has a set of human-like ears. Entreat God to send you a sign. You can simply say something like, "Guide me, Lord, give me a sign. Please Lord, send me guidance. Please hear me. Please guide me."

The American Indians express humility in their relationship with the Divine. They view themselves as children and always turn to their External Father in prayerful supplication. They ask for guidance knowing that some omen will certainly appear. The sign you ask for can materialize in any number of ways. It can be a body sensation which comes during a meditation. It can be a vision, a voice, an emotion or a rush of energy.

When you are consciously seeking guidance, let go of any preconceived model of how it should manifest. Someone's action, a printed word leaping from a page, a bird flying overhead, a dream or a song can all serve to guide. If you are *paying attention,* you will recognize the sign when it appears. Your guide may come in a form unique to you and never before experienced by anyone else. You will know it as Truth by the relaxation you will experience in your body and spirit.

8

TRANSFORMING
HUMAN EXPERIENCE

If you are earnest in your commitment to growth, the way you approach living should be completely supportive of your spiritual evolution. Right diet, right action and right company are vital areas of which to be conscious. This chapter contains information to serve you in creating a quality lifestyle which is conducive to transformation. In addition to useful information, it contains various tools and practices which can enhance your progress as you journey on the path up the Continent of Human Games.

Right Diet. When you are modifying your habits and routines to create more quality in your life, be sure to examine your usual diet. Your diet, just like everything else, should be in harmony with growth. It should reflect self-love and nourish you fully.

Therefore, all destructive and poisonous substances should be systematically phased out of your eating patterns. Refined sugar, coffee, alcohol, chlorine and chemical preservatives are dangerous to health and should be recognized as the toxic substances they are. Though you are not your body, it is nonetheless the vehicle in which you travel. If you want your progress to move ahead unimpaired, you must take care of your chariot.

Paavo Airola's books, *Are You Confused?* and *Hypoglycemia,* are excellent manuals on diet modification, exercise and cleansing fasts. They are also comprehensive guides to food supplements and other areas of health which can be extremely useful to seekers of Truth.

A survey of people growing in consciousness would reveal that by and large their diets are quite simple and composed primarily of unprocessed fruits, grains and vegetables. As people evolve spiritually, meat and dairy products sometimes drop away from their diets. Don't *force* anything out of your meals. Let items be eliminated as a result of actually losing your desire for them. Self-imposed austerity of diet creates an emotional block of resentment which may slow down your spiritual growth more than eating steak three times a day.

Right Company. Imagine living in a huge city with millions of people. At five o'clock rush hour, the underground subway system becomes unbearably congested. You arrive at a subway entrance ten minutes before five and descend several long flights of stairs. As you puff your way around a corner at the base of the last flight, a sign appears: ''This entrance closed. Use entrance across the street.''

You think, ''Certainly there must have been a similar sign at the top of these stairs. The wind probably blew it away.'' With a few deep breaths, you resolutely prepare for your ascent. Halfway up the stairs, however, you encounter the five o'clock rush hour throng pouring down the tiled stairwell. Thousands of people are descending and you try to tell them that at the bottom of the stairs the subway entrance is barricaded. It's hopeless, of course. They swarm past you like an army of ants.

At this point, you find it quite difficult to proceed with your ascent. In fact, not only is it hard to move forward, you might even feel that it is more sensible to turn around and move in the direction of the masses, even though you know it's a dead end.

The imagery here points to the advantage of being in the company of people who are heading in the same direction you want to go. Surrounding yourself with the right company is extremely important, especially when you are just beginning the journey of personal development. When you associate with people who are critical of your practices and are unsupportive of your desire for spiritual evolution, you are placing yourself at a severe disadvantage. A healthy environment is as important as healthy food.

When you plant a small tree it is wise to erect a fence around it so that animals don't eat it and people don't inadvertently trample it. When the tree grows large enough, then the fence can be removed since it can easily stand on its own. Care for yourself in a similar way.

Support yourself by seeking the company of people who are also dedicated to spiritual growth. Join a meditation group or a consciousness-raising organization or create a community of aware friends to live among. By having a network of emotional support in your life, you will get touched and hugged and listened to whenever you need it.

Disassociate yourself from people who are constantly negative and perpetually destructive in their words, thoughts or deeds. Only after you regard yourself as a pillar of spiritual strength may you wish to return to that type of company, so as to perhaps show them a new way of being.

Right Action. Your actions always create reactions. This is a simple law of cause and effect. Once you take personal responsibility for creating your life, you must be constantly watchful that you don't create what you don't want through actions which will have negative repercussions. As you become more aware of your own thoughts and watch yourself talking and moving in the world, you will see a connection between what you sow and what you reap.

Loving people seem to live in a friendly world and angry people seem to live in a hostile world.

There was once a fellow named Ron who in the 1960s wore a black leather jacket and associated with young men who always had an aura of contempt about them. One day, for whatever reason, he decided to change his ways. A group of "flower children" were having a musical "be-in" at the park when Ron appeared in his black leather jacket. Like a Saint Bernard puppy, Ron bounded up to the group shouting, "Love! Peace!" and waving his hands in the "V" sign that was a fashionable symbol for peace in the decade of the 60s.

The group of gentle young men and women upon whom Ron intruded thought him to be insincere and reacted to his awkwardness with suspicion. Despite initial rejection, Ron persisted in "acting" like the person he wanted to become. His actions were initially feigned, but in time he was no longer just pretending to be a loving spirit; he actually became one. Ron evolved into a radiant young man who gently moved through life spreading joy and harmony as he went.

The story of Ron shows how acting in a new way, even if awkward at the beginning, will eventually lead to the desired results. Actions are like magnets. They draw to us people and situations which vibrate in sympathy with the movements we ourselves create. Whatever you do comes back to you, regardless of whether your actions are negative or positive. You will be serving yourself greatly by remembering this always.

Simplification. Simplify your life. Why burden yourself with the stress that accompanies mortgage payments you can't really afford emotionally, revolving charge plans and expenses resulting from costly playthings? As we grow in consciousness, material possessions become less and less important. Simplification of lifestyle, just like simplification of diet, produces optimum health. Examine your life and see how you can simplify it.

There's a tremendous danger in using money as a measure of success. Many people have allowed the quality of their lives to deteriorate because their financial prosperity has misled them into believing that they were "winning," when they were actually "losing." Should a person consider himself a success if he has earned several million dollars, but his diet, personality and lifestyle have resulted in his having ulcers, hypertension, cardiac deficiencies and miserable relationships? You can use love, joy, nurturing friends, laughter and spirituality as far more accurate measures of your success.

Because Westerners have been intensely conditioned to equate monetary gain with success, we have compromised our entire culture by polluting the environment and destroying the minds and morale of countless millions. So long as the economy prospers, our governments tell us there is cause for celebration. Nonsense! Through simplification of lifestyle and a reordering of your priorities, you can create a Divine experience every day. Once you realize how little money is really needed to survive, you can spend more time dancing, running through the forest, hugging your neighbors, meditating and praying. Never confuse quantity with quality.

Devotion. Adoration feels good. When we worship a human form, whether it is our marriage partner or a deity, it opens our hearts. Several world religions focus on human forms as objects of worship. Tremendous feelings of love are generated by this practice. Devotion to a guru, a saint or the Invisible Spirit all produce similar results.

Try praying before a human picture which you particularly love. It can even be a photograph of a favorite grandmother. You will discover that the image on the photograph will have an effect on you. It will trigger an inner experience of love that literally seems to warm your heart. Once you find the right picture or pictures that create this feeling in you, place them in one area of your home. Use this same area every time you meditate or pray.

After a while, as soon as you sit in that spot, your body will relax and you will start to feel good. It will become a place of healing within your home. Oftentimes people on the path of spiritual development create a special room just for meditation or a small altar in some corner of their house. If you feel drawn to do this, it will enhance your devotional nature and will nourish you on a very deep level.

Conscious Breathing. Your breath is a vital link between your body and mind. Many therapies, including Bioenergetics and *Hatha* Yoga, use breathing to cause a mental change. *Pranayama* is the Eastern study of breathing as a path to enlightenment and has been used for thousands of years.

It is obvious that oxygen influences the mind. Pilots are required to use oxygen masks to insure the proper oxygen balance in their blood when flying at high altitudes. Judgment is impaired and reality distorted as ethyl alcohol replaces oxygen in our bloodstreams when alcoholic beverages are consumed.

Deep breathing can have a soothing and healing influence on your body and mind. When you are under stress, your breath shortens and becomes shallow. When thinking of an incident from the past that produced discomfort, you might even find yourself holding your breath. At those moments, a number of deep inhalations slowly released will ease the tension in your body and have a soothing effect on your mind.

Our breath has an unusual relationship to our past. From that first breath at birth, it's been our constant companion and was affected by every incident that caused our programming. It's obvious that on this path, we want to bring our unconscious patterns and habits to consciousness so we can transform them. Your breath can be the link between your present behavior and the past incident that caused your programming.

This quality of the breath is best tapped by continuous deep breathing. To do this properly, allow between half an hour and two hours; lie in a comfortable and quiet place where you know you won't be disturbed. You can do this alone, or ask a friend to sit with you for support and encouragement. Start to breathe deeply. Allow your breath to be one continuous motion; no pause between your inhalation and exhalation. Fill your chest completely and then exhale fully. Realize that as the oxygen level in your blood changes due to deep, rapid breathing, you might experience some dizziness or other unusual sensations. As the biochemical changes start taking place, muscles will sometimes tighten or cramp. This is not unusual and there is no need for alarm. Just keep breathing. Be conscious of memories, thoughts, feelings and sensations moving through you.

This simple process leads to insight and clarity, besides causing eventual relaxation in your mind and body. It also frequently taps into the Universal Bliss that surrounds all the human games. Doing this once or twice a week will have a very healing effect on you and will lead you into a more conscious relationship with yourself and the world around you.

The chemical change which happens in your body as a result of intense, prolonged, deep breathing opens up blocked channels of energy and makes reprogramming considerably easier. Sometimes, the breathing requires a strong commitment; especially if you have to get past dizziness or nausea which might happen. It is advisable to do this on an empty stomach; early morning is ideal. Expect some unpleasant sensations initially, so that if they occur you don't get discouraged. Two hours of conscious breathing will do remarkable things for your spiritual evolution. If you experience discomfort, remember that it is temporary; but your transformation will be permanent.

Right Thinking. The most important tool to use in growing spiritually is consistent optimism and positivity. Even when diet and exercise are deficient, right thinking can maintain perfect health. A positive mental attitude can keep you looking young and radiant when others your age are old and wrinkled. There are no limits to this power.

Above all else, rely on positive thinking as your vehicle for attaining your goals—nothing is strong enough to resist you when you keep your mind focused on love and success. Instead of lamenting that roses have thorns, why not rejoice that thorns have magnificent flowers adorning them? Replace your doubt with positivity and you will notice immediate changes in your experience of life. Research has clearly shown that our entire body chemistry can be changed with our thoughts. *Pay attention* as you think!

9

FOUR STAGES
OF GROWTH

If you become dissatisfied with the old ways in which you lived your life, spiritual evolution may have a chance to transform you. According to Marilyn Ferguson, author of *The Aquarian Conspiracy*, four distinct stages characterize this transformation that often occurs.

I. Entry Point. The first aspect or stage of growth is simply called *Entry Point*. This is when you first glimpse an alternative reality or realize that there was something false and unacceptable about the way you had been living previously. It can be stimulated by any number of situations. A friend may say something which strikes a chord of truth; or perhaps you have a near-death experience. An insight may strike you from nowhere. A book or hallucinogenic drug may jolt you into a new perspective on life. Whatever the means, *Entry Point* catalyzes a change and marks the beginning of a new growth pattern.

Imagine this rather extreme example. Suppose Mr. Jones, a middle-aged bank president, accidently ingests a sizeable dose of L.S.D. which his teenage son had inadvertently left on the kitchen counter. All of a sudden, he looks out the window and sees that the trees are breathing. He senses that he is one with all life and when he looks at the cat, he instantly feels he can read his pet's mind. All this, of course, is a striking contrast to his prior experience.

When his "trip" ends, Mr. Jones can pretend that it never happened, he can have a nervous breakdown or he can choose to further explore these radical new perceptions. He can even do all three: first deny his experience, then have a breakdown and finally choose to attempt making more discoveries. If he elects to continue pursuing these new ideas, Mr. Jones will pass into the second aspect of development known as *Exploration* or *Education*.

II. Exploration. This second phase of growth is the stage of continuing education. It is characterized by reading books, consulting gurus, taking classes, studying healing techniques, meditating, etc. Insight after insight will occur to you as you begin opening like a flower unfolding its petals.

Frequently, we believe we have attained ultimate "enlightenment" and are "finished." Yet, in time, we discover we can still develop more. Growth is much like peeling layers off an onion. A complete layer covers yet another complete layer. The process of cultivating self-awareness is infinite. There is no "end." An entire lifetime can be spent in *Exploration*.

Like the *Seven Life Requirements*, these stages of growth are not delineated by hard and fast lines of division. They entwine and overlap. Therefore, you need not remain in stage two before proceeding into the third phase of growth. Interestingly, the first two stages consume energy and the last two release energy. Until you have learned enough, it's difficult to outflow much energy. Self-development is a process of give and take. In the early stages of becoming aware, it is perfectly natural to want to take in as much as you can. At a point, however, you start wanting to give more. This taking and giving of energy is also true about the *Seven Life Requirements.* The first three consume energy and the next four liberate energy.

III. Integration. As you progress with your education, you will finally become conscious enough to notice when there are contradictions in the way you live your life. Obviously you want your outer life to be in harmony with your inner beliefs and you want your behavior to reflect what you've discovered in your quest for Truth. In other words, as aware beings, we feel a need to eliminate contradictions between our words and deeds. We wish to stand as examples for others to follow.

This stage of development is the phase of *Integration. It is here that we ourselves start becoming part of the solution* and not part of the *problem* on earth. In fact, if you aren't part of the solution, you *are* the problem. You can't extol the virtues of eliminating pollution and not recycle your own glass and aluminum. You can't preach love to others and hit your children in the privacy of your own home. Like Ghandi, you begin realizing there can be no difference between what you practice and what you preach.

A woman once asked Ghandi to tell her child to stop eating sugar. He replied, ''Come back in three weeks.'' When the woman returned with her son in three weeks, Ghandi simply said to the boy, ''Stop eating sugar. It is very bad for you.''

The woman was confused as to why he made her wait three weeks before admonishing her son to eliminate sugar from his diet. ''Because,'' Ghandi said, ''three weeks ago *I* was still eating sugar.''

As we move into the area of *Integration,* our thinking becomes more and more positive. Our actions too become more and more positive. Instead of seeing a glass as half-empty, we see it as half full. Optimism becomes a part of our very nature and it not only enhances our own lives, but also the lives of those with whom we associate.

IV. Networking. This fourth stage of transformation

coincides with the fourth Life Requirement. It is sharing. We join into a network with others by being willing to reach out and hold hands with our neighbors for the purpose of sharing our time and skills. We flow our energy outward and allow others to reap the benefit of sharing in our resources.

Each and every one of us has some skill or experience we can share or teach. If you doubt that you have valuable resources you can share, consider the story of the tent-maker's daughter. She was a woman about twenty years of age who felt that her father was depriving her of all hope for the future by demanding that she stay at home and work with him in his basement enterprise of making tents. She felt she was really a worthless dullard who had never been given an opportunity to develop skills or knowledge which would help her create a better future for herself.

Finally, after bitter years of resentment, she decided to run away from home. It was a daring thing to contemplate in the tumultuous times of the 15th century. But one night, while her father slept, the young maiden crept away into the forest. She had not gone more than a few kilometers when suddenly a bandit gang of gypsies and pirates seized her. She was summarily bound and tossed into a large basket on a mule cart.

After being jostled and bounced throughout the night, she was loaded aboard a ship in the early morning hours, still imprisoned within the basket. The next day she was deposited on an island shore and her captors departed.

The tentmaker's daughter was not alone on the island, however. The bandits had also left another prisoner, a young prince from a wealthy kingdom to the south.

The prince wailed, ''We're doomed. We're doomed. They've gone to blackmail my father, the King. But I know my father well. He will never yield to their threats and pay ransom for me. He is a hard, old man and they will surely return to kill us or leave us here to die of starvation.''

The tentmaker's daughter immediately knew what had

to be done. She dashed into a wooded grove and gathered saplings that she broke off with her bare hands. She had done it for so many years while making tent poles for her father. She tore her dress and the prince's shirt into strips of fabric that she used to bind the poles into a crude raft. Using her undergarments, she succeeded in improvising a sail using skills she had learned making tents. Soon the primitive craft was seaworthy and the two prisoners made their escape.

We don't know exactly what happened between the young prince and the tentmaker's daughter during the ten days they spent together sharing in this ordeal, but after returning safely to his father's kingdom, the prince and the young maiden were wed. The tentmaker's daughter was now a princess and would later become the Queen.

From this we see that no matter who we are, we all have something we can share. Look around and see where you can make a contribution to the expanding network of people serving people. You may choose to work alone or you may seek others to work with. Even in rural areas you can find kindred souls with whom you can share energy advancing the common good.

Before continuing with this idea of *Networking*, let's digress for a moment to consider an ancient tale about a prosperous king. The monarch was seated on his throne when suddenly his wiseman, who was also his right arm, burst into the room quite upset. "Sire," he began, "there has been a blight which has affected all the crops. Anyone who eats any of this year's crop will go insane. Fortunately, Sire, I have stored enough of last year's grain for you and me."

The king responded instantly, "Nonsense! If everyone in the kingdom is to be mad, why should we not be a part of them? We too shall eat the blighted crop."

To commemorate this decision to be one with his subjects, the king placed a mark on both his forehead and the forehead of his wiseman. "This way," said the king, "as we dash about in the madness, each time we chance upon each other, when we see this mark, we'll remember that we are crazy.''

This story about the "mark of madness" reminds us to look for those kindred souls with whom we can vibrate in harmony. Years ago, many people responded to the call of the New Age by rejecting old ideas and lifestyles, growing their hair long perhaps and donning frayed denim garments as a declaration of their distaste for established beliefs. Their ''mark of madness'' was readily apparent and those wearing it could spot one another without effort. Today, however, the "mark" is not so obvious. Proponents of the New Age dress in three-piece suits, uniforms, stylish polyester and many other "invisible" costumes. It is not so easy to spot them merely by noting the clothes they wear.

Yet if you truly desire to network with people of like mind, your sensitivity and persistence will reveal to you the others in your community who wear the same "mark" as you. Seek them out and immerse yourself in relationships which nourish you and encourage you to merge with the wave that is washing away old forms of living, old forms of government and old ways of thinking so that the New Age can thrive and people everywhere can live in the light of love and peace.

The survival of planet Earth literally depends on this new way of being. The old way was to take, take, take and take more. The new way is to *take less, give more.* The New Age Network is a leaderless society which may ultimately replace the existing forms of government. Government as it stands now is anti-people and anti-love. As people realize that they can provide for themselves that which no government has ever succeeded in providing, political institutions may crumble and one universal network of enlightened humanity might eventually inherit the earth.

In the final stage of growth, each person begins to take personal responsibility for the whole world. You yourself can make a difference. You are not powerless to change the planet; in fact, *YOU* are needed. *Your* love will help solve every problem in the world. Conversely, every time you react to someone with anger, *YOU* are responsible for every war being fought. As each of us takes full responsibility for the planet, never again will someone be able to see another person toss litter on the ground without bending down to pick it up. If you see someone litter and fail to clean it up, it is the same as if you threw that garbage yourself. *YOU* are the solution to every problem.

Earth is everyone's responsibility. If the liver has cancer, the eye can't say, ''Well, it's not my problem.'' We are all connected. Pollution and war on one part of the planet affects us all. We can't bury toxic chemicals and nuclear waste in the earth thinking we've discovered a garbage can. There is no garbage can. We *live* in the garbage can. Everything eventually seeps into the water table. *You must start seeing the planet as one organism* and seeing yourself as only a cell. If the planet doesn't make it, none of us makes it. The final stage of growth manifests as personal responsibility and unites you with every other conscious being on earth. Welcome!

Part Two

APPLICATIONS

10

OVERCOMING FEAR AND LIMITING BELIEFS

You can have whatever you want in life once you realize that *you create your own reality.* Your reality is simply constructed with beliefs. If you wish to change your reality, just change your beliefs. As it says in the Bible, "as above, so below." Whatever pictures you hold in your mind will be reflected in your life.

If you experience living in a very limited reality, where scarcity is common, it is because you have a belief system which is based on "lack." If your life seems to hold little satisfaction or reward, your mind process is causing that experience. There is no reason for some people to perceive abundance everywhere and others to find life a struggle except for the fact that some folks think "big" and others think "small."

Beliefs, like all other mind patterns, are conditioned programming and can be changed. Followed by doubt, the belief which limits us most and causes the most pain, frustration and failure, is FEAR. Fear should be first and foremost on your list of things that you might wish to reprogram. If you are willing to confront fear, you will discover that for the most part, it is only *False Evidence Appearing Real* . . . F.E.A.R.

An example of fear merely being *False Evidence Appearing Real* can be found in the tale about a man who was petrified of snakes. All his life, this fellow trembled at the very thought of a snake. One day, while vacationing at a mountain resort, someone casually said to him, "One has to be very careful in these parts, there are poisonous snakes *everywhere.*" Needless to say, this made the man feel quite uneasy.

That night, the man returned to his room after dinner and while fumbling for the light switch, there in the darkened chamber he saw a snake lying on the floor coiled and ready to strike. His fear grew so intense that it literally overwhelmed him and he had a heart attack. Clutching his chest, he fell to the floor dead.

The next morning, the man was found lying sprawled on the floor next to a rope. No one drew any connection between the man's death and the innocent rope coiled next to him.

What killed this man? Was it the rope? Of course not! What killed him was F.E.A.R.—*False Evidence Appearing Real.*

Our fears are constantly turning ropes into snakes. All fears have the same effect on us whether they are fears of animals, insects, heights, confinement, fears of failing, fears of succeeding, fears of rejection, speaking in public or any other situation. Fear limits! If you have unresolved fears, you never fully relax because you're never sure when circumstances will be such that the thing which stimulates fear in you will arise and suddenly you'll be out of control.

The best way to overcome fears and all other limiting beliefs is to confront them directly by being willing to examine them. A lady who moved to California from Ohio had a fear of spiders. Suddenly she discovered that black widows were a part of the natural environment around her new home. She instantly realized that she really had very few options in this situation. She could either sell her house or work on her fear.

Her approach was simple. She resolved that she would overcome her phobia by tackling it head on. She decided to take up a new hobby: the study of spiders. To know something is to be free of it. She went to the library and got several books on the subject of arachnids. She also wrote to several sources requesting information on the subject. She decided that each time she saw a spider, she would force herself to get close enough to examine it with a magnifying glass so that she could accurately determine its exact classification and species.

Through her own process of *Attentive Awareness,* she was able to discover that spiders eat insects and not people. By examining her fear through confrontation, it eventually disappeared.

Another person had acrophobia. His fear of heights was such that whenever he found himself in high places, his knees began to tremble, his heart raced and extreme dizziness brought him to the verge of fainting. The man tried therapy, hypnosis and numerous other approaches in an effort to be free from this lifetime fear. Finally, the man elected to use confrontation as a possible way to rid himself of his paralyzing phobia. He enrolled in a skydiving class.

The class was a brief four-hour session, after which a plane flew participants to a designated area where they jumped out the open door with a parachute. As the man sat in the doorway of the plane, his fear mushroomed into full bloom. All his physical and emotional symptoms erupted. Determined to win in his battle against fear, the man began to *pay attention* to his entire experience by examining every detail.

When he paid attention to the thoughts in his mind, he discovered a little voice in his head saying things like: "What if the parachute doesn't open?" "What if you don't land properly?" "What if you get tangled in the lines?" "What if you don't jump in correct form?" "What if. . ." "What if. . ." "What if. . ." Suddenly he realized that all his body trauma was a result of two words in his head: *What if!* His fear was nothing more than *What if syndrome.* He screamed, "SHUT UP!" to the voice inside him and jumped out the door. Victory was his and he never again had any fear of heights.

The difference between an enlightened person and an ordinary person is not that the enlightened person never experiences fear. The difference is that the enlightened person does not regard fear as a barrier to action. Pay attention to your fear as if it were a counselor cautioning you to be alert and to use full awareness. In dangerous situations, fear can be your servant, rather than your master.

As you form a working relationship with fear, the anxiety which used to traumatize you will be transmuted into the sensation of exhilaration. Your body may still go through some tension, but your *experience* of it will be entirely different. Instead of it being perceived as pain, you will notice that it is more like *excitement.* All you need do is allow the sensations to be what they are and simply pay attention to them.

Fear, as well as all other physical, mental, emotional, and spiritual limitations, can be overcome by setting an *intention* to do so. A simple, but incredibly effective four-point system to obtain any goal, overcome any obstacle and be free of any limitation is this:

1. Honestly examine your present condition. Unless you are willing to acknowledge your limitations, they will never be resolved. Just like planning a trip using a road map, it will do no good focusing solely on your destination point unless you know exactly where you are as well.

2. Visualize what you want. Be specific as you set your *intentions.* If you want to lose weight, do not merely see yourself thin, but describe your weight to the *exact* pound. In your imagination, *experience* what it would be like to *already* have obtained your goal.

3. Choose a plan of action. Rather than passively dreaming about what it is that you want, plan a strategy that will enable you to physically obtain it. If you were assisting someone in finding an obscure location, you would probably draw them a map. This third procedure is really just making yourself a map. Logically examine the step-by-step process which will take you to your goal. You may start on this by going backwards: before such and such can happen, first this or that must occur. Before this or that, so and so . . .

4. Follow your plan of action. Once your map is complete, all you need do to arrive at your destination is follow it. Simply creating a strategy will not manifest results. It must be put into action; it must be followed. Leading a horse to water won't quench its thirst. It must actually lean forward and drink.

The lady who was afraid of spiders used this four-point system, even if not consciously. She first acknowledged her fear and realized she would have to sell her house and move if it was not overcome. Next, she imagined that it was possible for her to live there without any fear of spiders and made that her *intention*. She then chose a plan of action, and finally, she followed it. Following it may have been the most difficult part. The first time she actually approached a spider with her magnifying glass may have been the hardest thing she ever did in her life.

Often, following the plan is very intense. Jesus is an excellent example of someone who knew where he was, where he intended to go, created a plan of action and followed it. He must have known exactly where it would lead, and yet he committed himself to following his plan. Ghandi, Columbus, Joan of Arc, Helen Keller and Ann Bolin are also models of people who chose to *"go for it,"* so as to accomplish their goals. The final point in the four-point system frequently involves taking a risk. Risk-taking can create growth faster than perhaps any other route. "Nothing ventured, nothing gained" is an age-old adage that sums it up.

In your attempt to overcome fear and limitations, ask yourself, "What's the worst that can possibly happen?" Visualize the most horrible results you can. As you see these disastrous images flashing in your mind, simultaneously see yourself *accepting* them. Experience *in your body* what the sensation would be like if you were able to emotionally accept the unacceptable.

After you have an *experience* of being able to *accept the unacceptable,* implement the second part of this technique, which is, *expect the best.* Visualize that you have already achieved what you want. *Feel* the experience of "winning" in your body. Hold on to that sensation as you proceed to follow your plan of action. When you are emotionally prepared for the worst and yet you are expecting the best, your mind relaxes into a sense of having "all bases covered." Maximum effectiveness always results from maintaining this attitude.

Doesn't it always make sense to *expect the best?* Why *not* expect the best? Imagine going to a movie and finding the line extending halfway down the block. You can worry and fret that you may not get a seat and spend an hour suffering. If you finally do get seated, that hour would have been an unnecessary experience of hell. Conversely, if you spend the hour expecting the best and find that there are no more seats, are you going to say, "Damn, I just wasted a whole hour feeling good?" Of course not! It never makes sense to do anything other than *expecting the best.*

For centuries people feared that if they sailed too far on the sea, they would fall off the edge. Mankind believed for ages that the world was flat. *False Evidence Appearing Real* kept us from exploring the world on which we lived. Columbus had to persuade scores of men to put aside their fear and accompany him on his now famous voyage. He dispelled a belief that had controlled the human race since the beginning of time. By his example, we learn that once a belief is *demonstrated* as false, it can never limit us again.

After sufficient evidence proves our beliefs are unfounded, we can never go back to using the old beliefs. Many things which we believe are difficult may actually be quite easy once we learn a technique or see how it's done. Some things we thought were impossible might be discovered as possible. For example, it was once believed that man could never fly. Today, however, we can fly 300 people across an ocean effortlessly. It was also believed that man could not walk on fire without burning his feet; yet we now know that thousands upon thousands have done it.

Overcoming your old beliefs, your fears and your limiting programming is just a matter of setting an intention to do so. If you can conceive it, you *can* achieve it!

11

LIVING IN
RELATIONSHIP

Imagine a woman who contracts a rare illness for which there is no known cure. One day while sitting at home, the phone rings and upon answering the call, the woman finds that it is her doctor. The physician explains, "A new drug has been discovered which may save your life. It is in its experimental stage, but you are eligible to receive it. By my calculations, you must get the drug by noon tomorrow or else it will be too late."

The doctor's call is reassuring, but the clinic where the serum is administered is over a thousand miles away in a remote corner of the land where no plane service is available. Two trains, however, pass near the clinic. One train is a comfortable passenger train and the other is a freight and animal train with no passenger service. The train which is by far the more comfortable is not scheduled to arrive there until late tomorrow night. The freight and animal train will arrive before noon.

If you were this person, which train would you elect to take: the slow, comfortable ride or the fast, uncomfortable ride? Of course, if your life depended on it, you would take the fast train.

Working with or living with others or being in a marriage-like relationship is one of the faster ways to grow, but not necessarily an easy way. It involves constant work on one's self and an unbending commitment to growth. The analogy of the dying person and the two trains may be a bit farfetched, but given the world situation today, our survival may very well depend on how rapidly we grow in consciousness. One rather renowned guru just recently stated that he will no longer work with people who are not in a committed relationship.

Loners and single people sometimes fool themselves into thinking they are somewhere where they are not. A famous example is the yogi who spends five years in a cave. He absolutely glows with what he thinks is the purity of enlightenment. Yet after emerging from his cave, an old man in the marketplace accidentally steps on his toe and the yogi explodes with anger. He calls the old man a stupid fool and clouts him on the ear. Obviously he hasn't attained enlightenment if he can only manifest *non-reaction* in a cave and not in the marketplace.

Relationships are like sandpaper, they keep polishing you until there are no longer rough spots and you shine. The rough spots, of course, are areas of your ego that still haven't been reprogrammed. Your marriage partner may be used as a perfect mirror that constantly reflects back to you where you need to be working on yourself. A hermit could possibly never anger simply because he is constantly isolated from human interactions that can test him.

Relationships, whether they be marriage relationships, business relationships or any other, can certainly be a test. Yet they do not have to remain perpetually difficult. They only appear hard in areas where you resist growing. If you view your companions as your best teachers, they will always keep you in touch with how effectively your program of self-development is progressing.

Your relationships are another aspect of life in which your beliefs and programming are reflected. As you grow and let go of negative programming, your experience of your partner or your friends will change. People only mirror back to you your internal pictures about relationships, marriage, the opposite sex, commitment, or intimacy. Every time you react with anger, fear or express any unpleasant emotion to your marriage partner, business associate or friend, a memory from the past is being stimulated and there is a chance for growth.

Your relationships can be a continuous experience of the Divine, in form, if you are willing to change your conditioning. If you still carry resentment from a past experience, such as your father's lack of attention, that same complaint will most likely surface in your present relationships. Any time you catch yourself thinking—"He's just like my father" or "Women are all alike" or "Just like so and so used to act"—realize that you are in the past. A mirror is being held up for you and here is your opportunity to grow. It's your beliefs which are being reflected back for you tu look at. There is no reality beside the one that you are constructing yourself. Your relationship with your marriage partner, your beloved, can be divine only if you forgive and let go of the past.

The area where married couples seem to struggle most is: *"control."* Frequently, we try to control our spouse's behavior to avoid having our own areas of unconsciousness stimulated. If he or she would only "respect" our limitations, we can hide the fact from ourselves that we are refusing to grow here. The results of all this are power struggles, arguments, manipulative game-playing and a lot of blaming.

Whenever you blame your spouse, your boss, your parents, friends or anyone else, it is only because you are feeling like a *"victim."* This is an indication that you are not taking personal responsibility for creating your own experience. When you finally remember that you are not a robot and that by using a reprogramming technique you can be free of automatic responses, the other person no longer has to be blamed or attacked with anger. As you yourself become more conscious, your anger at others does not have to be expressed or repressed, it can simply be *experienced*. As you grow in *understanding*, your anger will turn into *compassion* and love.

When someone "pushes your buttons," remember that you are being shown where you need to grow and learn to say "thank you." What may initially appear as a painful experience can soon be perceived as a gift if you are truly committed to evolving God-consciousness. The conscious person in any relationship is always the one who is more flexible and *yielding*. It takes *two* people to have an argument; if you wish to put out a fire, take away the fuel.

A poem to use as effective programming in relationships goes like this:

> He drew a circle that shut me out,
> But the power of Love gave me strength to win—
> I drew a circle that took him in.

If you consciously choose to view your relationships as a context for growth, then *anything* which transpires in a relationship becomes acceptable. You can let go of judgmentalness; you can stop judging yourself as well as your companions. After all, most actions are merely an outgrowth of the past. Since it is impossible for you to fully know someone else's entire past, you can stop taking their behavior so personally. It is only a result of their programming. If someone rejects you, it does not necessarily mean there is something wrong with you. You may be an absolutely perfect "plum," but there is always going to be someone who is allergic to plums. The American Indians remind us that we can never know why people behave as they do: "You can't know another person unless you have walked in their moccasins."

A simple exercise you can do in a few minutes goes like this. Take a sheet of paper and place the name of a person with whom you are having a relationship at the top of the page. Draw a line down the length of the paper so as to divide it into two columns. At the top of one column place a plus sign (+) and at the top of the other column place a minus sign (−).

Under the plus, make a list of all this person's positive qualities. They may include such things as generosity, honesty, tidiness, cheerfulness, compassion or whatever else strikes you favorably about them. When you finish this list, go to the minus column and itemize those things you characterize as negative aspects of this person's personality. These may be tardiness, fault finding, stubbornness, dishonesty, stinginess or anything you experience as "not good."

When you have completed the process, cross this person's name off the top of the page. In its place, write your own name. You will now have an accurate picture of the traits and qualities in yourself which you like and don't like. The only thing we ever see in someone else is a reflection of something within ourselves.

To illustrate this, consider this true example of two brothers who attended a party together. After the party was over, one brother said to the other, "That new fellow who just moved here from Chicago sure is arrogant."

The second brother reacted with total surprise, "You mean Frank? Arrogant? You've got to be kidding; he's so sweet. I thought he was a great guy."

The second brother did not have so much as a speck of arrogance in *his* nature, and so he failed to even recognize it in anyone else. The first brother, who had lots of arrogance in his character, instantly got to experience it by projecting it onto Frank. We cannot recognize in another something which is not in our own experience.

Suppose you see a woman shoplifting. Does it mean you are a shoplifter because you recognize it? Well, what if people from Mars descended to earth and viewed this same situation. They would just see a woman putting an item in her purse. No judgment would go along with viewing the action. You may not shoplift, but through society, parents or television, you have been programmed with pictures about shoplifting. If those pictures were not put into your filter system, you could not possibly see "shoplifting."

Your intimate relationships are like mirrors and provide the best possible opportunity for your growth by allowing you to constantly confront areas in yourself which limit you and need to be reprogrammed. Even if two people who live together are not both committed to growth, the one who *is* can rapidly evolve by using the other as a "teacher." It only takes one conscious person to make a relationship work, since the one who is conscious can learn from everything and anything the other one does.

The goal in relationships, of course, is to constantly experience people as God, the Divine Beloved. Whenever you are not having that experience, you get to see where your work has to be done. The process of being in relationships brings you closer and closer to discovering Divine perfection manifested in human form.

Like in the classic relationship of Rhada and her Krishna, you can learn to worship your playmates with complete devotion. This is the age where the rule for relationships is the same as the rule for living in general: pay attention more to what you are giving rather than what you are getting.

12

MERGING WITH GOD THROUGH *TANTRA*

Tantra is one aspect of Eastern philosophy. It is a way of merging with God through the technique of *paying attention*. In this instance, God is defined as *all that is*. *Tantra* is an experience and cannot really be studied. Words can point the direction of the path, but unless you actually practice it, *Tantra* will remain a mystery.

The first premise in *Tantra* is that you must accept *yourself* as you are right now. If you cannot accept yourself *as you are*, you will not be able to accept anything else without conditions. *Tantra* demands that you reject *nothing!* There is no such thing as an "ideal," there is only *what is*. Learn to welcome *every* experience and *pay attention* to it. Selectively rejecting *or* accepting only certain experiences retards transformation. The approach of unconditional acceptance eliminates the habit of *comparing* one thing with another. Everything just is what it is.

In essence, *Tantra* and *Attentive Awareness* are one and the same thing. This particular route of expanding awareness can actually be quite simple. It is a method which anyone can use regardless of intelligence or spiritual attainment. It represents a place from which to start and can be used immediately, even by beginners on the path of growth. All you must do to begin practicing this technique is to give up all your opinions. Neither judgmentalness nor discrimination is needed in life; simply make *everything* special or *nothing* special. In this way, all limitation is removed from your ability to experience.

This enables you to *harmonize* with everything and everyone in your environment. Since love is just an ability to accept unconditionally, you actually *become* love in action. *Paying attention* and *accepting* are not passive disciplines, they are completely active. Paying attention *is* a way of expressing love.

Attentive Awareness can be characterized as an ability to *surrender*. Surrender in this sense is not like military surrender that symbolizes defeat. On the contrary, in this case surrender represents victory . . . ultimate victory. You "give up" nothing when you "give in." Begin surrendering to the sky, to food, to sounds, to flowers, to everything. If you practice *Tantra*, it will transform you.

One of the unique aspects of *Tantra* philosophy is that it specifically instructs us to apply the principles of *Attentive Awareness* toward our sexuality. The reason for this is obvious. Sexuality and spirituality are completely entwined. Through the sex act, God manifests life and awareness on this planet. God, The Great Mystery, can be approached through conscious examination of sexual energy. By exploring sex with the intention of developing spiritual awareness, you can discover God.

Another reason to use sexuality as a focusing point for spiritual evolution is that it holds so much pleasure; there is a built-in incentive. Using sex as a tool for raising consciousness immediately demonstrates how easy and enjoyable paying attention can be. You can use lessons learned from sexuality by applying them to every facet of life.

A wire does not create electricity; it merely *conducts* it from the source. Likewise, we can draw the analogy that a sperm and an egg do not in themselves cause life; but, rather, their union *conducts* life to earth from the Source. After the sperm and egg unite, one complete cell results. This cell becomes two and then the two become four. The process continues until a human being finally manifests. Since every cell of your body comes from these sex cells, clearly, you are a sexual being and every cell of you is a sex cell. If you are to understand yourself, you must understand sex.

You may actually know very little about sex unless you have explored it through *Tantra* or a similar technique. Traditional sex is a mere extension of our day-to-day personalities. We simply carry our usual behavior into the sex act. If we are violent, or if we worry, or if we speed through our daily routines, this is exactly the way we behave when we get into bed. From now on, try getting into bed with a shift in energy, just as when people go into a church they allow their energy to shift. Approach the love bed as if it were a temple. Treat it with reverence and respect.

Every human being is created from a sperm and an egg. The sperm is male and the egg is female. Therefore, *every* human being is half man and half woman. Do not regard yourself as "any" man or "any" woman. Create yourself as the *only* man or the *only* woman. In this way, you can proceed with innocence and not let the mores and beliefs of society affect you. Pretend that civilization does not exist and that you are the original male or original female. Use affirmations to help create a positive mental attitude about your sexuality. An example of some practical affirmations are: "I am perfect." "It is Divine and it is safe for me to be sensual." "Sex is a loving and joyful expression of who I am." "I can express both my masculine and my feminine nature."

Remove all restraints on yourself when embarking on

the journey of sexual self-discovery. Do not *try* to be different than you are and do not strive to be some contrived ideal character. *To know who you really are, set aside all restraints and be who emerges.* This applies to all areas of life. Enjoy life. Don't force yourself to sacrifice. Sacrifice sometimes creates frustration and repressed anger. Serve *yourself.* Your actions, even those which are supposedly ''selfless,'' *are* really ''selfish.'' After all, when you do good or serve others, it feels good to you too.

As we proceed with our examination of *Tantra,* we will begin with sexual *Tantra* and then expand the philosophy to encompass all life. Finally, *Tantra* will be considered solely as a spiritual practice that results in what mystics term ''enlightenment.''

Tantric sex is a ritual and involves time. Do not plan to attempt *Tantric* lovemaking unless both you and your partner have allowed hours of time. Usual sex lasts between a few minutes to an hour, but *Tantric* sex can involve several hours, sometimes five or six, in fact it can last all night.

If you are planning to spend a *Tantric* evening with your partner, it may resemble the following scenario. Dinner is prepared with extreme love and care. The meal is consumed slowly with flowers and candles decorating the environment. Every glance toward your partner transmits your love and every gesture is already an act of lovemaking. The evening is dedicated to worshipping your beloved as God in form.

After dinner, you and your partner bathe together. The water may be perfumed and candles, fruit, flowers, incense and music can all be used to enhance the vibration of beauty and holiness. Each of you regards the other as a divine gift and appreciation for each other is reflected in each word and action. The bathing itself is an important aspect of preparing for lovemaking so that every body part is cleansed and annointed for your lover to worship and enjoy.

When you approach the love bed, you both give up any model or idea of what ''should'' happen. In this way, there can never be any disappointment. As thoughts move through your mind, just let them pass. Experience yourself as empty, much like a flute is empty until music results from air passing through it. Allow lovemaking to come *through* you rather than *from* you.

Ego is to be set aside as you and your partner get into bed. It is a time to lose your mind and come to your senses. Pay attention to your mate. Be as sensitive as possible to your beloved. Sit opposite each other on the mattress and gaze deep into each other's left eye. Massage each other. Allow your breathing to harmonize so that you are both breathing in unison: in together, out together. Let there be no more talking. Relax.

You and your partner are about to embark on a mystical experience. True love lies beyond lovers and in the process of performing *Tantric* conjugation, both of you may actually "disappear" into pure love.

At the appropriate time, when the penis is inserted into the vagina, the woman assumes the upper position. Traditional *Tantra* is usually performed with the woman lying on top or sitting in the upright ("Shiva/Shakti") position with her legs wrapped around the man's waist. With the woman on top, orgasm can be more easily forestalled. You are about to make love without any thought of climaxing. Pure *Tantra* is non-ending. The sex act is not a means to an end. The entire act *is* the end. There is no *momentum* as if it were going somewhere. Oftentimes, orgasm never occurs.

A stroll in the hills has no point of destination; you can return at any time. You are going, but there is no goal. *Tantric* lovemaking is similar in this way. It is always a "now" experience and is not seeking a final moment of climax. There is no "finish."

You surrender to your partner and you surrender to yourself. There is nothing to do, nothing to pretend. Let go and let God. Trust the wisdom of your body and don't hold back. Push nothing away and grasp after nothing. Be there as a witness to whatever happens.

After a while, imagine that you and your partner have no bodies; allow them to be consumed in love. Visualize yourselves as two souls. Finally, experience becoming one soul. No prior decisions are needed, just allow everything to evolve spontaneously. Let the sexual energy itself do the choreography, not the mind. Be in the sex act, but not of it. Just let it happen.

Experience one another completely. Do not just focus on erotic areas of your bodies. Let your energy rise so that every cell and pore of your being is stimulated by the ecstatic rapture of the Divine energy you traditionally term sexuality. Do not in any way feel self-conscious. Sometimes, you may wish to pretend you are alone. Touch the deepest core of your being as you permit your essence to be vitalized. Imagine that your partner is having the same experience.

When you first experiment with *Tantric* lovemaking, it may be difficult for the man to avoid ejaculating. Like anything else, practice is essential. The more frequently *Tantra* is applied to the sex act, the easier it will become. Two partners in a committed relationship can spend years developing *Tantric* techniques. There is no hurry; you both have the rest of your lives. Never bring guilt or a sense of failure into the love act because one or both partners attain orgasm. One secret of *Tantra* which helps control climaxing is long, deep, slow, easy breathing and periods of non-movement.

During intercourse, you are creating God. Lovemaking should be a holy ceremony which in itself is a form of meditation. It should leave each partner feeling calm and at peace. As you sit or lie with your mate, keep merging with whatever you are experiencing in the moment without any anticipation of what might follow. When kissing, *become* the kiss—not the kisser or the one receiving the kiss. This approach to sexual union will inevitably reveal many secrets of life.

As spirituality begins to consume your experience of sexuality, the man may suddenly sense that he is really a woman and the woman may feel as if she has become a man. When sensations like this arise, be aware of them without reacting. Constantly notice your own *awareness of yourself being aware.*

Sometimes a rush of energy will surge through your body, especially if intercourse is prolonged for several hours. Mystics refer to this as *kundalini.* If you and your partner make love sitting in the upright position with your spines straight, the *kundalini* energy may rise in response to deep, calm, rhythmic breathing. You may notice it as an inner explosion or as paralysis or as convulsions. This is temporary; surrender to it and taste the true wonder of egoless bliss. Knowing that this might occur reduces the chance of it startling or frightening you.

The exploration of *Tantric* lovemaking is a lifetime endeavor. During the early stages of discovering all aspects of your sexuality, orgasm will occur frequently. Orgasm itself should be experienced with complete *Attentive Awareness.* Notice that the orgasm is pure energy. Allow it to touch and excite *every* atom of your body. It is the outer manifestation of inner spiritual bliss. Experience the energy moving up through your body.

Sexual ecstasy implies or "points toward" Divinity. The "Cosmic Orgasm" is one which brings with it timelessness (nowness), egolessness and a sense of connection to the natural, *perfect* Universe. These three elements combined are the experience of *bliss.* Sex not only causes new life, but also renews the living.

Sexuality is a perfect symbol for God and must be explored *fully* if we are to use it for growth. Through the practice of *Tantra,* sex can literally take you *beyond* sex. You can extend lessons learned in the love bed to all areas of your life.

Anyone who suppresses sexual feelings will begin to

project them on everything and will often be preoccupied with them. They will be constantly busy with "not having sex." *Tantric* adepts are actually *less* sexual than repressed celibates because their sexual expression becomes transmuted into bliss; and bliss is *asexual*. True celibacy is not opposed to sex or opposite from sex, but only an absence of sex.

Tantra creates an environment in which enlightenment can occur. An example of this is the person who prepares for sleep. No one can say, "I'm going to sleep at ten" and simply lie down at ten and automatically be instantly asleep. Rather, we prepare ourselves for sleep by creating the proper environment: dousing the lights, quieting the room, reclining in bed. Sleep then comes to us of its own.

When enlightenment grows from the practice of *Tantra*, it is very gentle. It resembles the sun causing you to open your eyes in the morning after a night of being asleep.

Tantra is sex without mind. Mindlessness is always a confront to our egos. Therefore, ego-centered people will shy away from *Tantra*. It is such a childlike way of exploring sexuality. Our right hemisphere, which is responsible for intuition and creativity, is the only part of our brain that is ever employed in the type of sex now being described. You can experience sexuality playfully, with joy. You can be as spontaneous as a tiny baby in the love act.

Some people seek a more difficult path than *Tantra*, feeling that they need to struggle so that their egos can experience a sense of victory. It is ego which *seeks* power and respect, and yet, while the non-seeking of *Tantra* is the opposite of this, it is actually more powerful. The best way to be unharmed by a bullet is not with heavy armor or defense, but by "not being there." The bullet meets *no resistance* and passes right through.

Tantra is a path of no resistance. It is like an iceberg melting as it flows into the warm sea. Learn to welcome the experience of melting yourself in the sea of the love bed and in the sea of life. The greatest power is the power of knowing how to surrender. *Become* love; don't hang on to being one who practices "loving." Give up duality in the way you live your life. Do not separate yourself from that which you love.

Tantra allows you to *become* the Universe. Your body and smallness will dissolve. You can let go of thinking, since thinking separates the thinker from the subject being thought about. Oneness and wholeness result from learning to just *be*—you can feel *without thinking about feeling*. You can experience what it is like to be a liquid so that you are never separate from anything. You can flow *into* anything and anyone.

This way of being in the sex act actually removes "you" from the act. The "you" which constantly identifies with your ego, personality and programming has now disappeared. Even sex has disappeared. *Tantra* transcends "self" and suddenly your quest for self-realization is transmuted into true God-realization. You actually *experience* being God. You discover that *everything* becomes God through surrender. Surrender makes any relationship Divine. Sexual ecstasy can be found in any experience; meditation can be like sex without sex.

Frequently we encounter the phrase, "God is love." This means that *The All* is dissolved in oneness, merging, no separation, perfect harmony and acceptance of *All That Is*. The orgasm perfectly symbolizes this state. In a sense, *we are* God's orgasm, i.e., the experience God has of not being separate from every created thing. *Tantra* gives you a direct experience that God is love because you *become* all and accept all.

Once you master the essence of *Tantra* in your lovemaking, you can recreate the same experience alone. A partner is no longer needed because the entire cosmos now becomes your *Tantra* partner. Life itself is your beloved. *Tantra* or *Attentive Awareness* constantly puts you in the *now moment*. *Love* itself is a *now* experience.

God and love and time are all interrelated. In truth, time

is either past or future. "*Now*" is neither and is therefore outside of time. *Now* never passes and is thus a part of Eternity. It is always "*here.*" God too exists outside of time, always *now*. Eternity is not past and not future, rather, it is the everlasting point where they meet. We call it "*Now.*" Since love is in the *now*, love is eternal. This way of viewing love brings us in touch with the mystical quality of feeling aligned with something infinite and all powerful. Consciously making love in the "*NOW*" reveals God.

It has been said that *Tantric* adepts have a great sexual orgasm at their moment of death. Death brings the same experience as *Tantric* sex: timelessness (nowness), egolessness and instant connection to the natural, perfect Universe. These three combine to create the experience of bliss. *Tantra* enables you not only to have a better understanding of life, but of death as well. Both sex and death can be either struggle or bliss, depending on how you operate your consciousness.

Once you begin to *pay attention,* life becomes a celebration: true freedom. *Tantra* is a new way of living. When reading about it you might think that it is difficult; but you may find it actually quite easy. It is not serious, but playful. It allows us to be happy. As you use *Attentive Awareness,* you can change "poison" into "medicine." You can *use* anything. Everything can heal you.

Tantra is a way of living fully. Once the essence of *Tantra* is realized, even air becomes your beloved, even pain. There are no limits. *Tantra* allows you to say "thank you" to everything and experience *constant gratitude.* You can *become* the taste of food or *become* the scent of a flower. If you taste a raisin using a *Tantric* approach, your tongue can have an orgasm. It is all a matter of surrender; it takes *no effort.* If *Tantra* is your path, it should be easy.

Practicing *Tantra* is being already enlightened, just like practicing the guitar *is* playing the guitar already. Love is not a means to an end, it is an end unto itself. Let every experience *consume* you. The world *as it is now* is heaven, or as Easterners say, *Nirvana.* To deny the world is to never become enlightened. Each day can be an experience of heaven once you begin living with full sensitivity and awareness. *Attentive Awareness* can amplify pleasure into bliss and dissolve discomfort into God.

Let go of all your opinions about sex and *Tantra;* you have no opinions about eyes and no opinions about ears. Such should be the case with sex or anything else for that matter. All *Tantra* asks of you is to be more sensitive and more alive; live life *totally.* It is not a command to become an extremist, but even a path of moderation can include *excess* in *moderation. Life* is your chance to "go for it." Why hold back? Begin on the path toward heaven by *knowing you have already arrived.* Unlike traditional yoga, there is nothing to strive for with *Tantra.* In fact, it is exactly *non-striving,* it is *surrender;* it has been called "indulgent awareness."

Tantra is really making love with yourself. Your partner is a symbolic representative of *The Whole.* Use your partner to discover the secret of experiencing constant ecstasy. Once mastered, every waking moment can become *Tantra* for you. You can always be experiencing love, always be experiencing the True Beloved, always be experiencing God. No longer will you be moving *in* life, you will be flowing *through* it. Let go of control, even self-control . . . let go and let God.

13

PENETRATING
THE ILLUSION

Many people limit their experience of God with programmed ideas or concepts. Others reject the idea of God
altogether. Sometimes several different names are associated
with the Almighty; however, "a rose by any other name
would smell as sweet." If you feel resistant to the three-
letter word G-O-D, try putting your resistance aside so that
you may absorb an insight from the following pages. After
all, "something" exists which we perceive as the cosmos.
That in itself is worth exploring.

Can you imagine going into a gourmet restaurant, eating
a superb dinner and as the waiter presents the bill he says,
"Would you believe there's no cook?" The silliness of this
image is akin to denying that some process, by whatever
name, created all that exists today. To understand the process which has *caused* all "this," we have to perform "a leap
of the imagination."

In exploring the phenomenon which you know as the
material plane, both physics and metaphysics need to be
examined carefully. Therefore, some ideas may appear concrete while others seem abstract. In the end, all the loose

bits and pieces will be woven together. This demands your patience.

Two main points need to be looked at. The first idea is the concept of being one with God. How is it possible for a human being to say, "I am God"? We'll examine this point by reviewing one example after another of how the One can be many and how the many can be One.

The second idea explores the notion of our *reality* being nothing more than an illusion. Principles of modern science will be cited to create a point of reference from which to consider some radical observations of the Universe. Your mind may find the entire process exhausting, but your spirit will ultimately feel rewarded.

To begin with, let's look at the highly touted state of "oneness" that we hear so often in association with the New Age. A way of looking at oneness would be to draw an analogy using a symphony orchestra. The symphony itself is one vibrant sound, and yet, contained *within* it, actually *composing* it, are dozens of separate sounds emanating from various instruments. The whole, however, seems to be greater than the sum of its parts. Likewise, we experience that there is just one Universe; but it too is comprised of many parts: suns, moons, planets, gases, comets, you, me, him, her . . .

Another perception of oneness can be had by considering what happens when you inadvertently bite your tongue. While grimacing with pain, would it ever occur to you to get mad at your teeth? Of course not! Because it's *all* you.

When a glass prism is placed before a beam of light, instantly we see that contained within the white light is an entire spectrum of colors. Any physicist knows that white light is created by all the colors of the rainbow being merged. That is reality. As laymen, we get trapped in the illusion of believing that white light is an indivisible reality unto itself.

How you see something often depends on your perspective. You can point at the moon and ask, "What do you see?'' and get any number of responses including, ''a finger pointing.'' You can see millions of bubbles floating on the ocean and create an experience of viewing many things or you can create the experience of perceiving only *one* sea. Looking past your wrist you can either see five fingers or one hand.

Consider the illusion that the Earth is divided into parts. Children studying geography constantly see maps and globes which show boundaries and dividing lines across the planet. Yet upon taking their first plane ride, they can look down and immediately see that no such lines exist. Borders are manmade fabrications. The Earth is in fact one complete organism and it is only human beings that create the illusion of separation by dividing the planet into states and nations.

Trees, plants, animals and people are the sensory organs of the organism called Earth. You are constantly connected to this Earth just as if you had roots. Your skin and lungs are continuously linked to the living, pulsing bio-sphere. You need not limit and separate yourself from the planet by defining skin as a membrane which ''packages'' you into a tiny island or puddle of protoplasm disconnected from everything else. You can alter your perspective and see yourself as connected to all that is.

Imagine a tub of water in which ten empty bottles of different shapes have been immersed. If we liken ourselves to these glass containers we see that the same water flows in and out of each vessel. If we identify with being the bottles rather than the water, obviously we seem perishable. Yet if we view the glass sheathing as only that which defines us, i.e. personality, ego, programming and physical form, we can easily see that even after the glass is broken, the water, our essence, remains. The glass bottle is temporary and represents who we have been conditioned to believe we are.

As you become more aware you will begin to see beyond the apparent and sense another reality. Ten bowls of water will reflect ten images of the full moon. Growing in consciousness allows you to see that in reality, there is only one moon, even though everyone else claims there are ten. They keep pointing at the ground and counting aloud what their senses reveal. You are no longer fooled, however, as you discover that one Universe is constantly reflected in everything you encounter.

This way of perceiving life is a challenge, since the illusion of separation exists everywhere. Five blind men exploring an elephant "see" five different impressions. One believes the elephant resembles a tree as he feels a leg; another touches the elephant's side and claims it is like a wall. Since none of them are able to take in the wholeness of the pachyderm, their mistakes are inevitable. Likewise, we too usually experience the Universe in segments.

The "Universe" is a *concept* for unifying all the aspects and parts of the cosmos. Your car can provide another good analogy. There really is no such thing as a "car" *per se.* "Car" is only the *concept* describing all the assembled parts.

If you attempted to bring your car into your house, you might begin by carrying in the seats. Then you might bring the doors into the house. Item by item would follow: clutch, engine, tires, transmission, etc. Finally, you would go outside and there would be nothing left. Inside is just a mountain of parts.

Where's the "car"? "Car" merely is a *concept* for unifying all those screws, pulleys, valves and hinges. To extend the analogy further, there is no real "you" either; just a combination of *changing* behavior patterns, changing forms and changing cells. Every seven years, 95% of your cells are completely replaced.

Moving beyond the concept of being one with the Universe, we must start exploring the very nature of this Universe. Albert Einstein made one of the most startling discoveries when he found that the Universe was one unified field. This "substance" was at once both matter and energy. Until Einstein came along, physicists believed that matter and energy were two dissimilar entities. Yet if you've seen pictures of a nuclear explosion, you know that matter is only packaged energy and can be instantly converted back into it.

In school, we are now taught that everything can eventually be reduced to particles. Depending on how compactly the particles are compressed, we perceive either a gas, a liquid or a solid. By increasing the space between the particles of a solid, it can eventually fill any size space. As a gas, the mass in your body could be spread over the entire galaxy . . . a particle here, a particle there. The particles can be fragmented into sub-particles too.

When these particles are bundled close together, they appear to be at rest, since there is no perceptible movement. This "rest mass energy" is matter. Yet a lump of matter is still connected to the unified force of creation. Everything is.

In the laboratory, people have demonstrated rearranging atoms with their minds by materializing objects from air or by bending metal with their thoughts. It is possible because our minds are connected to the same force which causes everything to be. We are all the same "soup" and every fragment is still one with the whole. Using laser holography, a photograph can be reconstructed from any fragment, as each piece implies the rest.

Haven't you ever thought of a friend and within a split-second that friend called you on the phone? We may not yet have an intellectual understanding of it, but evidence of our interconnectedness is apparent everywhere. Our inability to explain so many phenomena is only because we are still limited in our studies of Mind and Physics.

Everything on the Earth came *out* of the Earth. No one dropped anything here by parachute. Each chair, house, factory, plant, animal and stone came *out* of the Earth. Scientists tell us that our planet is at most five billion years old. Then where was all *this* six billion years ago?

One theory is that the Earth came out of the sun. In

that case, the Earth and everything else, including ourselves, is solidified sunlight. Sunlight does in fact sustain us. Plants photosynthesize sunlight and store its energy and then we absorb it by eating the plants or by eating animals that eat the plants. We renew ourselves by taking in sunlight. We survive the cold winter by using fuels such as oil, coal or wood, which are also just packaged sunlight. We need not look far to be reminded that our source is light.

It took science centuries to puzzle-out "light." It has been thought to be a wave, a pulsing quantum, a vibration and a spiral. Even today, there are mysteries yet to be discovered in the properties of light. Ancient mystics often claimed that light had consciousness. No one can disprove them. Perhaps it's more than coincidence that within ENLIGHTENMENT is the word LIGHT.

A startling fact of today's physics is that no scientist has ever *seen* particles that compose an atom. We draw pictures of what we think atoms look like, but sub-atomic particles have never actually been seen. Physicists can view energy patterns with an instrument called a cloud chamber, but seeing a motion which "suggests" something is quite different from seeing a solid particle. After all, an air gun delivers a missile of air which on impact behaves as if it were quite solid; nonetheless, there is no-thing there.

Electrons, protons and neutrons may not be solid particles, but only energy patterns that behave *as if* they were solid. Their motion is bound tightly together in a package we label an atom. To date, there is *no* physical evidence that the reality in which we live has any more substance than sunlight. Our impression of every solid substance may be an illusion.

We are surrounded by illusions. Time itself is an illusion. We believe that time is a moving entity which approaches like a locomotive on a track coming closer and closer and then passing into the distance. In truth, time has no movement at all; it is always simply *"now."* However, we have invented clocks and calendars which fabricate units of measurement. Hours, days and months are purely man-made constructions of the mind. In reality, they don't exist. Time is a continuum; it is we who have fragmented it into segments for a matter of convenience. Again, we've become trapped in an illusion.

In elaborating on his theories, Einstein also said that nothing in the Universe is constant. In his equation $E = MC^2$, he used C to represent a constant. Since he observed that nothing is really constant, he put the speed of light in his equation as "C" becuase the speed of light *behaves as if* it were constant. Mathematically, it can be predicted when light will arrive at a given point; yet its speed actually varies, slowing up and accelerating as it travels. Even at this most basic level, we find that life is not constant.

Einstein further explained that everything is relative. An 80-year-old man sitting in a room with a five-year-old boy has a different *experience* of time. For the boy it moves slower, for the man it moves faster. Relativity also explains why ten people can give ten different explanations about how an accident occurred that they all have witnessed. Again we see how *perspective* colors reality. Everything observed is influenced by the observer.

All this implies that the "concrete" Universe you seek to label "reality" may not be so concrete after all. Reality may be a very relative, personal thing which anyone may perceive from an equally valid point of view. Fortunately, reality does not depend upon us agreeing with each other in order to exist. Reality, God or the Universe, whatever we choose to call it, is an *infinite* force. However, your mind is *finite:* it cannot even count the number of numbers. Obviously, something infinite cannot be measured with a finite instrument.

Therefore, your mind can *never* understand God. It is only if you surrender to this that you can experience peace. Someone once made the clever observation that Life is just an experience and anyone who reduces it to a matter of being "understood" deserves the "booby prize." The Great

Mystery is like an unwritten number, everywhere at once across all time and space. It will *never* be discovered with the mind.

Does all this mean that your quest for God is a hopeless treadmill? Only if you use your mind as your sole tool for discovery. It is possible though to have a *direct experience* of Reality. Once glimpsed in this way, however, it cannot be talked about, because then the mind would again come into the picture and distortion would take place.

It is also time that we start expanding our thinking to include more than one plane of existence. Before birth we had a *prior state*. Before any material object is made manifest, it exists as an idea; it has a *prior state*. Are ideas "real"? When Beethoven discovered his Fifth Symphony by hearing it inside his head, wasn't it just as real existing there as when he transcribed it to paper? Are dreams "real"? Are images we see in our imaginations "real"? The answer to all these questions is *yes*. "Reality" has several dimensions.

When you look at a tree you might be convinced that the tree is real. But look at what you're labeling "tree." Your experience, which you call, "that tree out there," is really just a bunch of electro-chemical synapses in your brain. What you experience as being "out there" is really an experience *in your brain*. In fact, every sight, sound, smell and perception of the world is only an experience *in your brain*. You only perceive what goes on inside your head.

The stars are not "out there," they are inside your brain. You have absolutely no idea what exists "out there." The only thing you ever experience is what goes on in your cranium. What you term "The Universe" is an experience you personally are having *inside*. *You* literally *create* what you are calling "The Universe." When you die, you take *that* Universe with you. *There are as many Universes as there are beings to create them.* The Great Mystery is not "out there," it is "in here." Your body itself is just your thoughts in a form you can "see."

What you are calling Reality is only a movie screen upon

which *you are projecting* images. The *source* of these images is *you*.

You are obviously connected to the "Whole," whatever it is. If you are only a *portion* of the Whole and yet you possess intelligence, imagination and an ability to dream, then obviously the Whole, of which you are only a part, is also intelligent, has imagination and an ability to dream. The One Mind certainly can do anything you can do with your mind.

When you dream about Tommy or Sally or Jim, it is always *you* listening through Sally's ears and looking through Tommy's eyes. Yet Tommy and Sally and Jim *don't know that*. For them, the experience they are having is "reality." Well, it *is* a reality, but only relative to the dream. Also, Tommy can never die because Tommy was never born. Tommy exists only in your mind.

What do you think it would be like for the One Mind to have a "dream"? Consider the possibility that *we* are characters in a dream *right now*. If we call the One Mind "God," then it is God looking through *your* eyes and God listening through *your* ears. Our present understanding of birth and death in no way contradicts this possibility. Our own dreams may provide a great clue to unraveling the Divine Mystery. Scientists have never seen solid particles at the core of the atom. How could they if it is all a dream . . . all Light?

This way of perceiving God is quite ancient. Thousands of years ago mystics referred to "reality" as an illusion. They concluded that "this" was but a mere dream. As characters in a dream, they also recognized that we are at once the dream *and* the dreamer. It is not possible to separate one who is dreaming from the dream he is having. That which we call the Creation is not separate from that which created it.

If it is God who is the Dreamer and if it is us in the dream, then we can choose to identify with being the tiny character in the dream or God who is having the dream.

We can shift between being that which is watched and being the Watcher. Since reality is so very relative, we can create it however we want. Whatever we believe becomes Truth for us.

Eastern philosophies suggest looking within as a route to penetrating the illusion via meditation. The Judeo-Christian Bible says, "Be still and know I am God." Each time you say, "*I am* doing this or *I am* going here," look at who this "I am" is that is speaking. In every moment that we are aware that we are aware, God is having an experience of being God in His creation. This God which you have always sought is none other than you yourself.

14

SERVING YOURSELF
BY SERVING OTHERS

You are capable of experiencing such an incredible amount of love. That is really what this book is about: bringing you to a place where you can realize that love is absolutely the most phenomenal thing that exists. Compared to love, all else in life becomes a footnote. As God, you have the capacity to enter into a relationship of love with everything and everyone. Love can make your existence a constantly rewarding experience of satisfaction and fulfillment. Why settle for less?

After you have passed through all the human games on the continent of life, you won't be bothered by the pettiness that prevents most people from being continually loving. You will have a perspective in living that will make each day an exciting new challenge for creating abundance, joy and excellence, not only for yourself, but for everyone else on the planet as well. This is what results from knowing who you are and that you have everything you need. When you discover your connection to the Infinite, what else is there to do but share? As you open yourself to love, it will flow from the Infinite Source *through* you, then on to others. Just as a tube is constantly cleansed by water channeled through it, you too will be vitalized by love as it is channeled through you on its way to serve humanity.

True love is compassion and it manifests in outflowing to people who are in need. Right now, the very planet itself is in need and must be healed by those of us who are capable of love. We *must* love . . . it's the *only* solution to the world's problems. No conscious being can look around, see what's happening on the Earth and say, "It's not *my* problem." If the Earth doesn't make it, none of us are going to make it.

Look around and see where you can serve. It *feels* so good. St. Francis said it beautifully, "It is in giving that we receive." His prayerful words are worth remembering as often as possible: Make me an instrument of peace. Where there is hatred, I will sow love. Where there is doubt, I will sow faith. Where there is despair, I will bring hope. Where there is darkness, I will make light. Where there is sadness, I will bring joy. May I not so much seek to be consoled as to console; to be understood as to understand; to be loved as to love. For it is in giving that we receive. It is in pardoning that we are pardoned. It is in dying that we are born to eternal life.

Today, 80 percent of the world's resources are consumed by 20 percent of the people. That is utter insanity. Why should 80 percent of the people struggle to get by on the remaining 20 percent of the resources? There's no shortage of *anything* on this planet. There's no excuse for hunger. The only reason for this imbalance is greed, unconsciousness and lack of imagination. *Now* is the time to start taking less and giving more. Earth can be heaven; but first some radical changes must occur. *You* are the instrument of the great change that is about to dawn.

A Sufi tale talks about a man who constantly prayed, "Show me the way to succeed in life." One night he had a vision in which he was told to spend the following day in the forest. So the next day he wandered through the woods looking for signs or omens. Finally, he saw a fox with no legs lying under a tree. Curious as to how a legless creature could survive, he hid behind a nearby stone to watch. Soon a lion came and laid some meat before the fox.

"Ah ha," the man thought. "The secret must be to completely trust that God will take care of our every need. I must stop seeking to provide for myself and surrender to the all-sustaining Lord." So the man sat himself down under a tree and waited.

After ten days, weakened and disheveled, the man had another vision. In it a voice said, "Fool. Be like the lion, not like the fox." The moral here again reminds us that all disaster needs to flourish is for good people to do nothing.

Imagination can guide you to serve in the highest way you can. Two brothers each inherited several million dollars. Both wanted to use their money to do good. One brother gave all his money to worthy charities. The other brother built a factory which was environmentally perfect and non-polluting. He trained unskilled people and created careers for them. In the long-run, his action may have performed a greater service than his brother's action of giving money to needy people. Everyone doesn't always choose the same path.

There are several schools of thought in Buddhism. One, called *Hinhayana*, teaches that our highest goal should be to realize our inner God-nature and immerse ourselves in that divine bliss. Another school, called *Mahayana*, instructs that bliss cannot be enjoyed if all around us are people suffering. For them, bliss follows serving the human family of which you are a member.

If you were of the *Hinhayana* school, after wending your way up the Continent of Human Games and discovering the Sea of Bliss at the northern shore, you would jump in. If you were a *Mahayana* Buddhist, upon reaching the shore, confident that you yourself now knew the way, you would return to the Garden of Sharing so as to point others in the right direction. Only after you yourself were too old to effectively serve would you return to the Sea and jump in.

We live in an age which cries out for more Buddhists

of the *Mahayana* philosophy. Any good deed or thought you can send forth to create healing is needed desperately right *now*. Whether or not we are to survive as a species will be determined before the close of this century.

Fortunately, more and more people around the globe are waking up to the healing power of love. Instead of war, competition and separation of power, they are striving for unity, sharing and peace. Everywhere we look we can discover people who are starting to align with the ideas expressed in this book. As a race, mankind is beginning to experience the phenomenon of the "hundredth monkey syndrome."

The story of the hundredth monkey refers to an experiment conducted by a group of Japanese scientists. They put a supply of sweet potatoes on isolated islands inhabited only by monkeys. Observation revealed that on one island a young female monkey would always wash her potato before eating it. Soon her siblings also began washing their potatoes. Next her playmates joined the ritual. Soon, the parents of the young monkeys were washing their potatoes. Gradually, more and more monkeys were washing their sweet potatoes before consuming them.

After about a hundred monkeys were predictably washing their food before eating it, a very interesting thing happened. One morning, *every* monkey on the island began washing their potatoes. The incredible aspect of the experiment is that on the same day, on every other island, *all* the monkeys began washing their potatoes as well . . . even on islands where no monkey had ever washed a potato.

This experiment led to further research on the idea that when enough minds focus on one thing, minds everywhere are affected. When a certain specific gravity is reached in one area, it seems to alter the whole mass. Scientists have just recently discovered that a child can learn a poem much faster if it is a rhyme that children have been reciting for several generations. Though they themselves have never heard it before, children are able to memorize traditional poetry several times faster than similar poems which have been contrived solely for the experiment.

These investigations reveal a new hope for the future. When enough of us begin to use love and spiritual awareness as a guide for living, the whole world will be affected. It is not necessary to reach every human being on the planet for the New Age Network to succeed. All we need are a hundred monkeys. In fact, *you yourself might be that hundredth monkey.*

AN INVITATION

Imagine you are incredibly hungry. You walk into a restaurant, sit down at a table and the waiter immediately appears with the menu. It is a glorious menu indeed. Each delicacy is exquisitely described in glowing detail and several of the entrees are pictured in brilliant, full-color photographs. The waiter leans forward saying, "May I suggest this," and as he does so, he tears a picture from the menu, sprinkles it with salt and offers it for you to eat.

The image here is of course absurd. Eating the menu will certainly not satisfy your appetite. There is no way to compare the description of food with the actual experience of eating it; just as a vivid description of skydiving will certainly not give you *the* experience.

This pocket-guide* is much like a menu. It briefly describes ideas and concepts presented in our 9-day Spiritual Reality Training seminar, commonly known as the S.R.T. If you found the subjects described here appealing, we invite you to join the S.R.T. and actually taste what it is like to live in a spiritual reality for nine days. The S.R.T. is a practical workshop which teaches how to interpret abstract ideas so you can directly experience them as real. Anyone interested in joining the S.R.T. can obtain a schedule of times and locations by contacting us through the publisher.

Much love to you,

Tolly Burkan
Peggy Dylan Burkan

Guiding Yourself into a Spiritual Reality has an accompanying workbook. The workbook is $6.95 and can be ordered by mail from Reunion Press. Add $1.50 for postage and handling.California residents add 42¢ sales tax.

SUGGESTED READING

The following books can greatly assist you in developing a strong foundation for spiritual growth:

1. *Are You Confused?* **Paavo Airola.** This is one of the best books on diet, nutrition and food supplements available today.

2. *Hypoglycemia.* **Paavo Airola.** This describes the symptoms and remedies for a condition resulting from poor diet and the over-consumption of sugar. It is *highly* recommended for everyone, especially parents.

3. *Handbook to Higher Consciousness.* **Ken Keyes.** This handbook has become a classic training manual for speeding the transition from old behavior patterns into expanded consciousness.

4. *How to Make Your Life Work or Why Aren't You Happy?* **Ken Keyes and Tolly Burkan.** This small book provides quick insights on how to stop creating unhappiness in our lives and how to produce happiness in its place. *(Available from Reunion Press.)*

5. *The Impersonal Life.* **Sun Publishing.** This is an *excellent* introduction to discovering how God-consciousness dwells within us.

6. *Creative Visualization.* **Shakti Gawain.** This collection of simple techniques and methods will assist you in creating whatever it is that you want and eliminating what you don't want.

7. *I Deserve Love.* **Sondra Ray.** This book provides effective methods for using affirmations.

8. *Dying to Live.* **Tolly Burkan with Mark Bruce Rosin.** This inspirational autobiography reveals how even the most intense suffering can change to joy. *(Available from Reunion Press.)*

9. *Be Here Now.* **Ram Dass.** This comprehensive collection of information on spiritual development contains many insights and ultimately opens the reader's heart. It presents an excellent perspective on devotion.

10. *Autobiography of a Yogi.* **Paramahansa Yogananda.** This awesome volume reveals incredible glimpses of magic and miracles while inspiring readers to pursue spiritual development in their own lives.

11. *Love is Letting Go of Fear.* **Gerald Jampolsky.** The *Course in Miracles* inspired this small book on how to use love as an approach to any situation.

12. *Aquarian Conspiracy.* **Marilyn Ferguson.** This is a rather academic book, yet it provides observations about the New Age which are startling, meaningful and relevant.

13. *Siddhartha.* **Herman Hesse.** This short novel reveals how the spiritual path may affect a person's life. It is very enjoyable reading.

14. *Stranger in a Strange Land.* **Robert Heinlein.** Although appearing to be science fiction, this enchanting and wonderful book reveals countless insights into the workings of consciousness and human behavior. It is also a fun book to read.

15. *Tales of Power.* **Carlos Castaneda.** This is one of a series that describes mystical experiences collected while studying with an Indian sorcerer.

16. *Jonathan Livingston Seagull.* **Richard Bach.** This short story has many levels of meaning. It is a book you will want to read over and over again.

You can be on our mailing list and receive notices about new books, tapes and special events by sending your name and address to Reunion Press, Box 1738, Twain Harte, CA 95383.

GUIDING YOURSELF
INTO A
SPIRITUAL REALITY
WORKBOOK
$6.95

ORDER FROM YOUR BOOKSELLER OR
REUNION PRESS
DETAILS ON BACK OF TITLE PAGE